THE CRESTA RUN

THE CRESTA RUN

by

N. F. SIMPSON

"Looking out of my window, one morning in late Autumn, I saw a little old lady of ninety-three doing the Cresta Run in a pony and trap. The memory of it has stayed with me ever since."

BARON BOLGERHAUSEN VON
TRITT-HEBBELSTEIN

FABER AND FABER

24 Russell Square

London

First published in mcmlxvi
by Faber and Faber Limited
24 Russell Square London WC1
Printed in Great Britain by
Latimer Trend & Co Ltd Plymouth
All rights reserved

THE CRESTA RUN

The first performance in Great Britain of *The Cresta Run* was given at the Royal Court Theatre on 27th Oct. 1965

The cast was as follows:

Leonard Fawcett	FRANK WILLIAMS
Lilian Fawcett	AVRIL ELGAR
Sir Francis Harker	SEBASTIAN SHAW
Timothy Cask	TIMOTHY CARLTON
Gelda	NERYS HUGHES
Andreyevsky Bolsover Griffiths	BERNARD GALLAGHER

The production designed by John Gunter
Directed by Keith Johnstone

CHARACTERS

Leonard Fawcett
Lilian Fawcett
Sir Francis Harker
Timothy Cask
Gelda
Andreyevsky Bolsover Griffiths

ACT ONE

ACT TWO

ACT ONE

SCENE 1

The Fawcetts' living-room. Night.
When the CURTAIN *goes up the stage is dark.*
A doorbell rings three times in quick succession and there are sounds of movement. Lights go up outside the room, and we hear someone go to the door.

LILIAN: (*off*). Whoever is it, at this time?
> *We hear a bolt being drawn and a chain being taken off the door. The light comes on in the living-room as* LILIAN FAWCETT *enters, switching it on. She is a slightly greying woman, apparently in her fifties, though she may well be anything up to ten years younger. She is in a dressing-gown and has her hair pinned up.*
> *The living-room has two doors. The one through which* LILIAN *has come leads in from the front hall and stairs. The other leads out to the kitchen and the back of the house.*
> *There are one or two pictures which hang by cords from a picture rail. Two armchairs, a table with two chairs at it, an open roll-top desk, and a rather ugly miniature grandfather clock.*
> *The carpet near the door to the hall is slightly curled up at one corner. Under it can be seen a layer of newspapers whenever someone kicks it up.*

HARKER: (*off*). Good evening. I wonder if I could

trouble you, at this rather late hour, Mr. Fawcett.

LEONARD : (*off*). Oh. Well. Yes. Come in.

HARKER : (*off*). I'm sorry to inconvenience you like this but . . .

We hear the front door close and immediately SIR FRANCIS HARKER *is in the room. He is a biggish man in his fifties, with a bluff, amiable manner.*

LEONARD FAWCETT, *who follows him into the room, is wearing a dressing-gown, and boots which he has hastily put on and has not had time to lace up properly. He wears these or carpet slippers throughout. He is a slightly shorter man than* LILIAN, *and though in his late forties, like her he looks about ten years older.*

SIR FRANCIS HARKER *accidentally kicks up the carpet as he comes in and pauses to straighten it with his foot.*

LEONARD : I must get that tacked down.

HARKER : Sorry to disturb you at this hour, Mrs. Fawcett. Something's turned up a little bit unexpectedly and I wanted to try and contact everybody as soon as I could.

LILIAN : Oh. . . .

LEONARD : This is Mr. . . . (*Reading from a card.*) Frank Harker . . . from the Intelligence. Wants to have a word with us.

HARKER : You know how it is in counter-espionage, Mrs. Fawcett. Every second counts . . .

LILIAN : I'm sure it must.

HARKER : . . . and we find ourselves in need of your co-operation—if I could possibly trouble you to that extent at this rather late hour.

8

LEONARD : Anything we can do. Only too glad to be of
assistance.

HARKER : Let me put you in the picture as briefly as
I can. What's happened very broadly is
this. Over the last few months one or two
of the big London stores have been
receiving orders for large quantities of
food. We've managed to track down some
of these orders, and they are without any
shadow of doubt for very large quantities
indeed. Seventy-nine pounds of rice,
eighty-seven tins of sardines, a gross of
potted shrimps, six hundred and forty-
three sticks of celery, a lorry-load of dried
apricots, things of that order. Sultanas,
cheese, biscuits. Everything you can think
of in fact in the way of food—except for
just one, rather significant, thing.

LILIAN : (*saying the first thing that comes into her
mind*). Caviare.

HARKER : Exactly. (*There is a slight double-take here
as he goes on without pausing but with his
eyes rather curiously on* LILIAN) Which, as
you know, comes from an unnamed
country on the other side of the Iron
Curtain—namely Russia.

LEONARD : What's going on then, do you think?

HARKER : Well—we can't as yet be absolutely sure,
of course, but we have reason to believe
that we're on the track of something pretty
big, and that's why we want to act as
quickly as we can. Because you see these
food orders are not the kind of thing you or
I would hand over the counter once or
twice a week. They're on a vast scale, and

9

any store receiving one of these orders would naturally get to work on it right away. They'd bring in people from other departments if necessary and work through the night. It would be a top priority job. No store worth its salt would dream of doing anything else. In fact they've had so many of these orders over the last few months that they're dealing with them like clockwork. Now. As long as the orders are for groceries in general, we're not concerned about it. But you can no doubt imagine what's in the back of our minds. All it needs is for someone to give the signal, and suddenly without warning every single order, instead of being for groceries in general, is going to be . . .

LEONARD: . . . for caviare.

HARKER: Exactly.

LEONARD: My God!

HARKER: And of course they'll be carefully timed to reach all the stores concerned within a split second of each other—so that before anyone really tumbles to what's happening the stuff will have been packed, loaded on to vans, and sent out. The vans will be hijacked, and when the drivers come to, every single scrap of caviare in the country not in private hands will have vanished into thin air.

LILIAN: Good heavens.

HARKER: We shall be literally drained of caviare at one stroke.

LEONARD: Which means, I suppose, that we'd be completely at the mercy of Soviet Russia.

10

HARKER: Who'd of course be able to hold us up to ransom for it.

LILIAN: You mean they'd actually do that?

HARKER: I'm quite sure they would. If they were allowed to get away with it.

LEONARD: In other words we should have to go to them cap in hand.

HARKER: Instead of negotiating for it from a position of strength as at present.

LILIAN: But they must be stopped.

HARKER: Well, this as a matter of fact is where you come into the picture, Mrs. Fawcett. And Mr. Fawcett too, of course. Because the names of the stores involved are known to us at Intelligence and Security Head-quarters, and are in fact on a list which we have and which I need hardly say would be of intense interest to anyone who could get hold of it; and not least to the gang who are behind this coup. In fact the chances are that they'll stop at nothing to get possession of it—if only in order to know how much *we* know. I don't have to tell you how absolutely vital it is that at all costs we prevent this list falling into the wrong hands.

LILIAN: Naturally.

LEONARD: Any help we can give.

HARKER: What we've done so far is this. We've cut this list into sixteen pieces, and placed each one of these pieces in a sealed capsule. *He takes it out of his pocket and shows it to them.*

LILIAN: That's something I should never have thought of, I must say.

11

LEONARD : It's very neat, certainly.

HARKER : It is, isn't it? Now what we'd like—if you feel you can do this—is for you to take one of these sealed capsules and secrete it for us in the hollow ballcock of your lavatory cistern.

LEONARD : I see.

HARKER : Do you think you could do that?

LEONARD : Yes. We'd be only too glad to. I'll go up and do it right away.

LILIAN : It's nice to know we can be of assistance.

HARKER : Well, it is a very great help when people do co-operate in such a friendly spirit, and we are most grateful. Not everyone is as ready to come forward and help us as you are by a long way. I expect I shall have one or two doors slammed in my face before I dispose of the rest of them.

LILIAN : Surely not.

HARKER : Oh—it's all in the day's work, Mrs. Fawcett. We get used to it.

LEONARD (*confidentially, as man to man*). I take it you don't want us to shout it from the house-tops or anything that we've got top secret material in our cistern.

HARKER : It would be better if you didn't. All helps to keep the security people happy, if you can manage not to let on to too many of your neighbours that there's anything going on of an at all hush-hush kind.

LEONARD : Quite. What's going to be the follow-up of this? If it's not an indiscreet question?

HARKER : It's not an indiscreet question at all, Mr. Fawcett. In fact I'm glad you asked me. It's just as well not to be too much in

12

the dark, in case anything goes wrong. As
it very likely will.

LEONARD: We'd better both listen to this, Lilian.

HARKER: What will happen is very roughly this. The
precise location of this capsule, as of the
other fifteen, will be known to only five
men. No one of these five is known to the
other four. Their first knowledge of one
another's identity will be when they meet
for the first time under the floorboards of a
typical suburban house somewhere in
Greater London.

LILIAN: I see.

HARKER: To which they will have gone—ostensibly
as pest control officers—to inspect the
joists for death watch beetle. Now. Each
of the five will have brought with him part
of a telephone handset—exactly similar to
the one you have yourselves out there in
the hall. These parts, when assembled
under the floorboards, will provide the
equipment necessary for making an
ordinary telephone call.

LEONARD: To Brixton, say.

HARKER: Yes—or Exeter. Dundee. Anywhere.

LEONARD: Quite.

LILIAN: If they can make it to one place, they can
make it to another.

LEONARD: Yes, I know. That's what I . . .

HARKER: Right. They will then stage a mock fight.
Under the floorboards. All but one will get
knocked unconscious, and this one will
promptly dial the secret number assigned
to him and ask for Bob. This will be the
signal to the operator to block all other

13

incoming calls for thirty-five seconds.
Among the calls so blocked will be one
from a special agent in West Hartlepool,
who will have been dialling continuously
every ten seconds for six weeks prior to this
moment.

LEONARD : West Hartlepool.

HARKER : Yes. Now, when he finds his call blocked,
he will act quickly, in accordance with
sealed instructions which he will have had
secreted on his person since the previous
October. What these sealed instructions
are, I cannot of course divulge, but what I
can tell you is that within a matter of
minutes a vast fleet of plain delivery vans
will be on its way, loaded with caviare, to
prearranged rendezvous in different parts
of the country, where government agents
will be ready waiting in secret hide-outs
to receive them. And so, of course, foil the
hijackers.

LILIAN : Well . . . I must say. It's certainly well
thought out.

LEONARD : Not very much left to chance.

HARKER : No—we can't afford to leave things to
chance, Mr. Fawcett. (*He gets ready to go.*)
And now I must be off to try and dispose
of the other fifteen.

LILIAN : Well—I hope you'll have every success.

HARKER : If everybody turns out to be as co-operative
as you and Mr. Fawcett, I shan't have
much trouble. But I'm rather afraid that'll
be too much to hope for. Don't bother to
come to the door. I'll see myself out.

LEONARD : I'll get this up there right away.

HARKER : Good. And thank you very much. Good night, Mrs. Fawcett, Mr. Fawcett.

LEONARD ⎫
LILIAN ⎭ Good night, Mr. . . .

LEONARD : (*with a glance at the card*). . . . Harker.

LILIAN : I'd better just go to the door.

We hear the front door open and close, and the sounds of LILIAN *locking, bolting, and putting the chain on it. When she comes back in, she pauses, as from long habit, to straighten out the carpet with her foot.* LEONARD *is still standing with the capsule in his hand.*

LILIAN : I wonder why he chose to come here.

LEONARD : Unless we've been singled out for some reason.

LILIAN : I do wish you'd get this tacked down, Leonard. I keep asking you. We shall break our necks one of these days. Besides letting everybody see what newspaper we've got under the carpet.

LEONARD is staring hypnotized at the capsule, which he has lying flat on the palm of his hand, while LILIAN *picks up* HARKER'S *card, looks at it, and props it up on the mantelpiece.*

LEONARD : Not very impressive, is it? Really? Hard to think that within twenty-four hours from now, we shall probably have every long-ranged rocket from here to Vladivostock trained on our lavatory cistern.

LILIAN : Yes—well, we'll worry about that in the morning.

They go out and LEONARD *switches off the light.*

15

ACT ONE

Scene 2

The Office. Morning. Some days later.

A large, imposing door at the back gives on to Sir Francis
Harker's *room. Two other doors connect, on one side with
an adjoining office, and on the other with a corridor. The
room is panelled and carpeted. In it is a leather armchair and
a large, moderately imposing leather-topped desk, which
is used by* Cask. *On the desk are several telephones, an office
intercom, and a terrifying piece of equipment in the form of a
box covered with locks, switches, signs, and warning lights.
Inside is the special phone which connects with the "hot"
line to Moscow. There is also on the desk a small wooden
card index, which is totally out of key with the impressive-
ness of its surroundings. In a corner of the office is a ticker-
tape machine, of the kind which pays out an endless strip of
tape at one side, and down left is a small, permanent film
slide projector, which throws a picture on to a small screen
built into the wall at the back.*

Gelda *comes in through the door from the corridor. She
is a girl of about nineteen, bright and chirpy, with an off-
hand but friendly manner, and an attractive appearance. She
looks round the room a little uncertainly, and then, with a
slight shrug, sits down in the armchair. She sits there for a
time, taking in her surroundings, waiting, spinning round in
the chair, looking at her watch. Then she gets up and goes
across to look at a map.*

Andreyevsky bolsover griffiths *comes briskly in from
the corridor. He is a small, lively, nondescript-looking man,
who could and does take on almost any appearance at will,
when required to do so for professional purposes. He is at
present dressed as an onion-seller from Brittany. He is
making for the adjoining room, and is more than half-way*

16

across the office before he sees GELDA.

ANDREYEVSKY: Hallo. What are *you* doing here? In the holy of holies. I thought you were still across the road. In International Secrets Exchange control.

GELDA: So I am.

ANDREYEVSKY: Till when?

GELDA: Officially till Monday.

ANDREYEVSKY: Then what?

GELDA: Confidential duties.

ANDREYEVSKY: Really? I say.

GELDA: If I like the sound of it. When I eventually find out what it is I'm expected to do.

ANDREYEVSKY: Is that what you're here for now?

GELDA: Half-past nine, they *said*.

ANDREYEVSKY: He's probably in with you-know-who.

GELDA *takes in* ANDREYEVSKY'S *disguise.*

GELDA: You're very security-minded, aren't you. Do you always come in like that?

ANDREYEVSKY: Second nature, really. You do it without thinking.

He goes through into the next room, leaving the door open. GELDA *wanders up to it in order to talk through it to him.*

GELDA: Then you go through there and take it all off again.

ANDREYEVSKY: That's the general idea.

GELDA: It seems an awful lot of houha.

ANDREYEVSKY: Just a precaution against being seen coming into the building and recognized.

GELDA: Why? Is that so terrible?

ANDREYEVSKY: You don't want everybody to know who you are.

GELDA: No, I suppose not.

She goes and sits down.

I hope he's not going to be much longer.
Pause. GELDA *surveys the room.*

Do you know what I'd do? If I were in
charge of this place? To liven it up a bit?
I'd throw it open to the public.

ANDREYEVSKY *appears at the door. He is
changing out of his disguise, and is in his vest*

ANDREYEVSKY : (*aghast*). You'd do *what*?

GELDA : Put people in the picture. Let them know
what's going on. I mean—nobody knows
anything about it, do they? It's all shrouded
in mystery.

ANDREYEVSKY : It's *meant* to be shrouded in mystery!

GELDA : But what's the good of its being shrouded
in mystery, if there's never anybody here to
see it shrouded in mystery?

ANDREYEVSKY *goes off, shaking his head.*

They talk about the general public co-
operating with the government to maintain
a high and stable level of national security
and all that, but they don't do anything to
arouse people's interest in what they're
doing, do they? They ought to have a great
big publicity drive. Don't you think that's
a good idea? Stir things up a bit.

ANDREYEVSKY : (*off*). I think it'll be a good idea when
you're packed off on to confidential duties.
And the sooner the better.

GELDA : It's not as if we get a look in at the Royal
Tournament or the Aldershot Tattoo,
even. Disguises Down the Ages. Followed
by that magnificent spectacle, The Grand
Musical Ride of the Mounted Doubles.
With a massed choir rendering popular

18

numbers between items from the Secret
Service Community Song Book. How
about that? Culminating in nine breath-
taking episodes from the Great Secret
Service Mutiny of 1873. When every plain-
clothes man in the service came out in
fancy dress. And the Head of Security
came out on to the battlements in a three
button dark grey worsted two-piece suit
and held the enemy at bay single-handed,
till the mutiny was quelled and the ring-
leaders hanged.

ANDREYEVSKY *appears at the door in
considerable alarm.*

ANDREYEVSKY : How the hell did you know about that?
GELDA : It's in the Handbook. The very stuff of
legend. Or whatever they call it. Don't tell
me you haven't read your Handbook. Tut,
tut.
ANDREYEVSKY : I've never heard of a Handbook.
GELDA : Handbook for New Entrants? Didn't they
give you one when you came in? All those
many centuries ago.
ANDREYEVSKY : (*going*). Handbook for New Entrants! My
God. What *are* we coming to?
GELDA : How did *you* find your way around then?
In those far-off days.
ANDREYEVSKY : We just had to come in and get on with it.
Nose things out as best we could.
GELDA : Yes. Well. We're all terribly mollycoddled
nowadays, you see. We have to have it put
on a plate for us. No initiative or anything.

GELDA *wanders over to the door and looks in
at* ANDREYEVSKY *for a few moments.*

I wonder what they'll want me to do.

Exactly. For confidential duties. Whatever
it is, it'll be an improvement on what they
give you to do over the road. Sitting all day
long in front of that dreary great computer
pressing buttons. Secrets In on one side,
Secrets Out on the other. It's not *my* idea
of a job in the Secret Service.

ANDREYEVSKY: It's vital work.

GELDA: I'm sure it is. It wouldn't be so bad if I
understood what I was supposed to be
doing.

ANDREYEVSKY: Well, unless you know how many of your
own secrets are leaking across to the other
side, and how many of theirs are finding
their way back to you, there's no way for
either side to know what the overall
balance of secrets is at any given time.

GELDA: I know.

ANDREYEVSKY: That's the whole *purpose* of the International Secrets Exchange Control. That's
what the daily index is for. So that if the
flow gets dangerously out of balance, it
can be regulated on the international
market. It's like any other form of export
and import.

GELDA: I wish I had your job. All these outside
assignments. Impersonating people, passing messages, stealing documents, tracking
down other agents.

ANDREYEVSKY: It's not all that marvellous.

GELDA: It's better than being cooped up in here,
anyway.

The door from HARKER'S *room opens and*
CASK *comes in.*

CASK: Ah. The very man. I was hoping you'd be

20

in. (*He sees* GELDA.) Miss . . . Crompton?

GELDA : That's right.

CASK : Yes, I'm sorry to have kept you waiting.
But I shan't keep you much longer. I'll
be with you as soon as I've got this last
little bit of routine out of the way.

GELDA : Oh. Not at all.

CASK : (*to* ANDREYEVSKY). Now. How do you feel
like ferreting something out for us in
Baluchistan?

ANDREYEVSKY : Not another foot-slogging job, I hope. To
Khartoum and back.

CASK : No. This is something nearer home. And
it's going to be a bit of a wild goose chase,
I'm afraid, but it can't be helped.

ANDREYEVSKY : Interflora?

CASK : That's right. It's beginning to look as if
they're on to Project Number One Death
Trap.

ANDREYEVSKY : Which is?

CASK : The new dual purpose concrete-mixer and
combine harvester being developed by
Tottenham Borough Council for use
under the North Sea.

ANDREYEVSKY : Aha. So my job is what?

CASK : Your job will be twofold. In the first place
we want you to get yourself fished up on
the end of a line off the pier at Brighton
under cover of an angling competition,
hitch a lift to Doncaster in an ice-cream
van, insert a small Black and Decker
rotary scythe with hedge-clipper attach-
ment under the dashboard, and lie low.

ANDREYEVSKY : And in the second place?

CASK : In the second place, and at the same time,

21

we want you to impersonate three six-foot guardsmen in quick succession while playing the bagpipes on the back of a motor-bike.

ANDREYEVSKY : Bagpipes? On the back of a motor-bike? No, thank you. I've had all the bagpipes *I* want. In Swansea.

CASK : Yes—well, I'm not pushing them, if you'd sooner chance your arm with something else. What do *you* suggest?

ANDREYEVSKY : If it were left to me, I think I'd as soon settle for a 1923 Sheraton-type twin-action harpsichord, frankly.

CASK : The good old standby.

ANDREYEVSKY : People sneer at it, but it's reliable, and it's easy to ditch if you have to.

CASK : True enough. Oh, and . . . I don't suppose you'll find yourself with time on your hands, but in case you do you might like to know that we've got someone on either side of the road from Torquay to Headingley with four spare sets of Winsor and Newton's Number Nine lino-cut tools.

ANDREYEVSKY : Good. You seem to have thought of everything.

CASK : We like to take as few chances as possible.

ANDREYEVSKY : Very considerate of you.

CASK : Especially when we're sending one of our best men on a fool's errand.

ANDREYEVSKY : So what do I do now? Go on down to briefing, I suppose.

CASK : Yes. I'll ring through now to let them know you're on your way.

ANDREYEVSKY: (*going*). Right.

CASK: Oh—and good luck.

ANDREYEVSKY: Thanks, and let's hope we end up this time with something more than the plans of the Victoria Embankment.

He goes to the door as CASK *picks up his phone.*

CASK: No call for cynicism.

He goes out.

(*Into phone.*) "Harry? . . . Cask here. I've just sent someone down to you. Andreyevsky Bolsover Griffiths, to be exact. . . . Yes. . . . Ideal for it, I should have thought. . . . Right. Splendid.

Now. Miss Crompton.

GELDA *sits opposite* CASK.

The reason I asked you to come across and see me was so that I could try and give you some idea of what the confidential duties are we wanted you to undertake. I think you ought to know exactly what's involved before you come to a decision. In the first place, of course, you won't be using your own name. For professional purposes and while you're on duty, we should want you to be known simply as Gelda. This is the name you would be using to clients, and that clients would be using to you. You'll find that in the main your clients will be drawn from embassy circles, chiefly foreign embassies, and from quite a number of different walks of life in other spheres as well.

GELDA: I see.

CASK: You might be asked to take on a Cabinet

23

Minister one day, and a visiting nuclear physicist the next. So it's varied work, and you would, of course, be broadening your background. And quite a number of girls look on it as an opportunity to improve their languages as well.

GELDA: What kind of hours would I be expected to work, Mr. Cask?

CASK: Oh—it's not arduous in terms of hours, at all, Miss Crompton. And your actual commitments would vary from week to week. At one time you might be attending to the needs of two or three clients one after the other. At another you might be cultivating one particular client over a period of time—in which case you would have to be prepared to place yourself at his disposal more or less at a moment's notice.

GELDA: Would there be anything to stop me taking on others, if I wanted to, in between times?

CASK: Not in the least. Provided it didn't interfere in any way with the work you're doing for us here. Anything else, of a freelance nature, would be up to you entirely.

GELDA: Yes. I suppose I'd be silly to let the opportunity go, really, wouldn't I?

CASK: And I need hardly say, of course, that you would be on a substantially higher salary rating than you are at present. And the premises are provided, together with everything you need—apart from the things you'll be wearing and any special equipment you may want to use. So you would be financially better off in every way. Not that that is necessarily the

primary consideration—but it's good to
know that one is earning a generous
remuneration for work which is at the
same time in the interests of the country.

GELDA : Do I have to try and get military secrets
out of them or anything, while I'm . . .
looking after them?

CASK : Oh, no. That's entirely our responsibility.

GELDA : I see.

CASK : We do all that.

GELDA : Blackmail them, I suppose.

CASK : Well—one doesn't like to use the word
blackmail in this context. We do bring a
certain amount of pressure to bear,
sometimes. In the interests of the greater
good. But that need be of no concern
whatever of yours, Miss Crompton, I can
assure you. You'd simply be required to
do your own job.

GELDA: I see. Well, yes. I think I'd quite like to do
it.

CASK : We'd certainly be very glad to give you an
opportunity of proving yourself. But we
don't have to have a decision right away.
Why not come and see me again, Miss
Crompton, when you've had a chance to
talk it over at home?

GELDA : (*getting up*). Yes. Well, I'll do that. And
let you know.

CASK : Excellent.

CASK *gets up to say good-bye to* GELDA.
Good-bye, Miss Crompton. And I hope
we shall soon have you on our strength.

GELDA : Good-bye, Mr. Cask.

GELDA *goes out.* CASK *returns to his desk.*

ACT ONE

Scene 3

The Fawcetts' living-room. Morning. A week later.
Breakfast. LILIAN *is reading the paper and* LEONARD *is emptying cornflakes from the packet on to his plate. A bright red plastic object falls out. He picks it up and looks at it with a sort of resigned gravity. It is a hammer and sickle.*

LEONARD : It's started.
LILIAN : What has?
             LEONARD *pushes the hammer and sickle*
             towards her.
LEONARD : It hasn't been up there a week, and they're
             on to us already.
LILIAN : What is it?
LEONARD : In the cornflakes. It fell out of the packet
             as I was pouring them.
LILIAN : It's only a bit of red plastic.
LEONARD : This is a good deal more than just a bit of
             red plastic, Lilian.
LILIAN : I can't see what else it is.
LEONARD : Look at the shape of it. There's only one
             thing that's that shape. And that's a
             hammer and sickle.
LILIAN : Oh. Well, I can't think how it got there,
             then. It was a new packet. Unopened.
LEONARD : They presumably have ways and means.
             Pause. They eat, and LILIAN *reads, in silence.*
             I suppose this is one of the things we can
             begin to expect.
LILIAN : What is?
LEONARD : This.
LILIAN : Oh.

26

        Pause.

LEONARD : From now on.

        Pause.

        It's happened to other people besides us.

        Pause.

LEONARD : Microfilm in the sugar bowl. Tape
        recorders under the brisket. That's going
        to be the pattern from now on. They plant
        them. To incriminate you. (*Meaning
        hammer and sickle.*) Like this. Pick up a
        spoonful of jelly, and before you know
        where you are, you're biting on the ultimate
        deterrent. An anti-missile missile.

    LILIAN : Not if you look what you're eating.

        Pause.

LEONARD : Miniature free-ranging microphones
        embedded in the gorgonzola. That's
        another dodge.

        Pause.

        A few crumbs of *that* lodging in a dental
        plate at ministerial level, and they're
        intercepting vital secrets a split second
        before they're uttered.

        Pause.

        There's no doubt about it. We're going to
        be in the forefront of the battle as far as
        intelligence and security's concerned, from
        now on.

    LILIAN : There's a boiled egg in the saucepan out
        there.

        LEONARD *goes out and comes back with the
        egg.*

LEONARD : That's one thing there's no doubt about.

        Pause.

        What does it say about the spy trial, then?

LILIAN : Apparently they got on to him when it
came to light he was buying both his
chauffeurs four new liveries a year out of
a part-time assistant furniture remover's
wages.

LEONARD : Getting money from the other side to do it
with.

Pause.

LILIAN : They've arrested that filing clerk. I see.

LEONARD : Which one?

LILIAN : At the . . . what is it? . . . Public Works
and Monuments.

LEONARD : Oh, yes.

LILIAN : Systematically leaking details about the
ventilating system at the Air Ministry.

Pause.

The things they'll stoop to for money.

Pause.

Chess-player.

LEONARD : Oh?

Pause.

LILIAN : Been losing his queen to a Russian naval
attaché every night for six weeks.

Pause.

If that's not a security risk, I don't know
what is.

LEONARD : Where's that card he left the other night?
With his number on it?

He goes to the mantelpiece.

LILIAN : Which card?

LEONARD : Here it is.

LILIAN : Oh, that one.

LEONARD : Security 9411. I think I'll get on to him.

LILIAN : Whatever for?

LEONARD : About this. (*Indicating the hammer and*

28

sickle.) Cover ourselves.

LILIAN: It's only a bit of plastic out of the conflakes.

LEONARD: I think it's something they ought to know about.

LILIAN: If it is, they'll find out of their own accord. That's what they're there for.

LEONARD: Yes—but . . .

LILIAN: (*getting up*). You're fussing again, Leonard. Sit down.

LEONARD: There's no harm in putting them in the picture, Lilian.

LILIAN: (*going out to the back*). They won't thank you.

He goes towards the door into the hall.

LILIAN: (*reappearing at the door*). Whatever you do, don't get us involved in anything.

LEONARD: I shall just tell them briefly what's happened. I'm not going to elaborate.

He goes out. We hear him dialling.

(*Off.*) At least it'll put us in the clear.

ACT ONE

SCENE 4

The Office. Same.

CASK *is sitting at the desk working. Suddenly a brilliant red light comes on on the "hot" line equipment followed by a rapid series of urgent high pitched whoops (which go on until he eventually picks up the phone). CASK leaps up like a man possessed, and goes madly through the drill for getting at the phone. It involves a complicated process of using an inter-locking series of keys all over the office, but although his knowledge of the drill is impeccable, one of the keys gets stuck and as a result the operation takes several frantic minutes. Finally, just before getting through to the phone itself, he operates a switch marked "failsafe", and then snatches up the phone. The whoops stop.*

> CASK: (*into phone*). Yes? . . . Yes. . . . Mr. Who? . . . (*He draws the card index towards him and goes through it as the name is spelt out*) Yes. . . . F . . . A . . . W . . . C . . . E . . . double T. . . . (*He finds the card and takes it out.*) Yes. . . . Yes. . . . Aha. . . . Yes. . . . I see. . . . Naturally. . . . You would have been. . . . Yes. . . . May I ask, (*referring to the card*) Mr. Fawcett, who gave you this number? . . . I see. And can you give me any idea what else you were told by this person, Mr. Fawcett? . . . Caviare. Are you quite sure caviare was mentioned? . . . I see . . . Yes. . . . Yes—well, if I could explain to you what I think may possibly have happened, Mr. Fawcett. When this person called on you, it was late at night, and you may not have noticed what was happening —but I feel pretty sure that in fact you and your wife must almost certainly have been looking, quite inadvertently, through the wrong end of a scrambler telephone. . . . Oh, yes, it does happen from time to time, and of course the impression you'd get would be somewhat misleading— intentionally so. In order to confuse any unauthorized person such as yourselves who might find themselves unwitting eavesdroppers. As seems to have happened

30

in this instance. . . . Not at all, Mr. Fawcett. I'm glad to have been able to set your mind at rest. . . . *That* I couldn't divulge, I'm afraid, Mr. Fawcett. (*He refers to the card.*) Quite out of the question. You can rest assured it was something quite harmless of a confidential nature.

. . . I'm afraid not, Mr. Fawcett. Only to full members and their accredited agents.

. . . In your where? . . . In your ballcock.

. . . Yes, that may well be true, Mr. Fawcett, but it wouldn't, even so, entitle you to more than associate membership.

. . . Well, yes—we do. . . . Certainly I will.

. . . I'll make a note of it now, and get it off to you right away. . . . Yes, if she wants to, she can certainly make application at the same time. . . . On the same form. . . . That's right—although I think I ought to explain to you that you would both be required to undergo a fairly rigorous programme of tests before being called for interview, and that full membership is conditional upon the successful completion of what many people might consider a quite arduous course of training. . . . It is, I'm afraid, Mr. Fawcett. . . . The only way.

. . . Yes. . . . Right. I'll do that, Mr. Fawcett. Thank you for getting on to us.

. . . Yes . . . Good-bye, Mr. Fawcett.

He puts the phone down and flicks a switch on the intercom.

VOICE : Yes, sir?

CASK : Get me everything you can on a Mr. and Mrs. L. J. Fawcett. Husband's name

31

Leonard. Wife's name Lilian. And send
them application form PKY for full
membership.

He flicks another switch.

Andreyevsky Bolsover Griffiths. I want
him on a new assignment. Now. Tell him
to drop everything and keep a twenty-four
hour watch on a Mr. and Mr. L. J.
Fawcett. Husband's name Leonard. Wife's
name Lilian.

HARKER *comes in.*

HARKER : Good morning, Cask. Anything in from
Q6 this morning?

CASK: Good morning, sir. Only this, I'm afraid, sir.
He hands a slip of paper to HARKER.

HARKER : (*reading*)' "Excuse scrawl. Gagged,
handcuffed, drowning. Trust all is well."
Helpful.
*He puts it down and crosses from force of
habit to the tape machine.*

CASK : I've just had a Mr. Fawcett through on the
hot line from Moscow, sir.

HARKER : What!

CASK : Something about a hammer and sickle in
his cereal.

HARKER : Who is he? Do we know him?

CASK : (*picking up the card*). This is all we've got
on him at the moment, sir. But I've alerted
special branch. We're having him watched.

HARKER : Who's our best man?

CASK : Andreyevsky Bolsover Griffiths, sir.

HARKER : Put him on to it.

CASK : Yes, I've done that.

HARKER : (*with card*). Do you know, Cask . . . this
rings a bell. . . .

32

CASK : Seemed to know quite a lot about
Operation Sturgeon Roe, sir.

HARKER : The devil he did!

CASK : He claims to have a capsule, or something,
secreted in the . . .

HARKER : . . . in the hollow ballcock of his lavatory
cistern.

CASK : Well—yes. . . . As a matter of fact.

HARKER *is plunged deep in troubled thought.*
The thing that makes it all the more
puzzling is that somehow or other he's got
hold of this number.

Pause.

Which means we shall have to ring round
all the embassies again and change it. The
Post Office will go up the wall, of course,
but that can't be helped.

Pause.

HARKER : I don't know whether you realize the full
significance of this, Cask.

CASK : I realize it's pretty serious, sir.

HARKER : Of course it is. But that's not the point.
The point is that in the whole of the
Ministry there's only one person who
could have given this number to an
unauthorized member of the public, Cask.

CASK : Well. . . .

HARKER : Because there's only one person who
knows it. And that's me.

CASK : You're not suggesting, sir . . . ?

HARKER : I'm suggesting nothing, Cask. At the
moment. Except that two of our most
closely guarded secrets have somehow or
other found their way into the hands of
someone who for all you or I know may be

working for every single damned alien power this side of Ribblesdale.

CASK : It's certainly a bit unfortunate, sir.

HARKER : It's more than unfortunate. It's downright disastrous. No good calling it unfortunate. It's the father and mother of a security breach, Cask. You know it, and I know it. *Pause.*

CASK : It's just one of those things, sir. It happens to all of us.

HARKER : It's happening to me a damn sight too often, Cask. This is the third time in six months. If it goes on, God knows where it's going to end.

CASK : There is one reassuring aspect, sir. If I may say so. Now that we know who it is, we don't have to bother keeping tabs on anybody else.

HARKER : That's the least of our worries, Cask. A breach of security is a breach of security. Whoever's responsible. It doesn't make it any less catastrophic because we know who blabbed.

CASK : What happened, sir? Were you . . . ?

HARKER : Was I what?

CASK : I just wondered what . . . whether it was that you'd . . .

HARKER : That I'd *what*?

CASK : . . . drunk too much at the time, sir.

HARKER : Good God, no, Cask. It just comes over me. At any time. I might be all right for months, and then suddenly I get one of these attacks. Out of the blue. And when that happens, all I can do is to pray that it isn't anything too vital that gets let out.

34

This time I seem to have prayed in vain.

CASK : What's the . . . cause of it, sir?

HARKER : Classic case of Bolgerhausen's multiple
allegiance syndrome, Cask. Mixed ancestry,
you see. Back in the time of Queen Anne.
The subconscious has never known for
for certain where one's basic loyalties
really lie.

CASK : Comes out in the form of subversive
impulses.

HARKER : Exactly, Cask. Which are the very devil to
control.

CASK : Couldn't you take something for it, sir?

HARKER : I wish I knew what, Cask.

CASK : One or two people I know have had a fair
measure of success with the Official
Secrets Act, sir.

HARKER : My dear chap. I've been signing the
Official Secrets Act night and morning for
the last five and a half years. That's very
much a broken reed.

CASK : Or there's naturalization, sir.

HARKER : Yes. Once every three years and a booster
every seven. It may come to that in the
end. But I want to steer clear of it for as
long as I can. People are very funny about
having the security services run by somebody who needs naturalizing.

CASK : True, sir.

HARKER : Bad for the image.

CASK : There is, I suppose, one small crumb of
comfort, sir. For what it's worth.

HARKER : Yes?

CASK : And that's that the Press have been on to
us for months for a grave security breach

they can denounce the government for.

HARKER: Yes. They have.

CASK: This should be just what they're looking for. Slackness in high quarters. Keep them happy for a month or two.

HARKER: It should.

CASK: Ease the pressure a little bit.

HARKER: Yes. You see, Cask, the thing that worries me is that it's been going on for so long. That's what worries me. It's not something new. It's something I've had all my life.

CASK: Yes, sir?

HARKER: I remember quite clearly as a small boy coming over subversive one day in Woolworth's. I was watching a girl serving someone with curtain rings at the time. Middle of the afternoon one summer. One moment I was feeling fine, not a care in the world, dipping into a bag of mint humbugs, unless my memory plays me false, and the next thing I knew I was struggling in the grip of an overpowering impulse to undermine the legally constituted government of the country in the name of an alien philosophy.

CASK: A hair-raising moment it must have been for you, sir.

HARKER: Not a very pleasant experience, Cask. For a small boy of nine.

CASK: It certainly wasn't, sir.

HARKER: To this day I've never discovered what brought it on at that particular moment— and of course within seconds it had passed. But it was by far the most nerve-racking experience, while it lasted, that I've ever

36

undergone before or since.

CASK: I can well imagine it was, sir.

HARKER: Terrifying. In fact you can imagine what it
was like when I tell you that during those
few seconds it was all I could do not to
turn to the girl behind the counter, beckon
her across, and divulge an atom secret to
her. And if by some catastrophic
combination of circumstances I'd happened
at that moment to have one on me—I
really think I might have done it. In the
middle of a crowded Woolworth's, with
every agent within earshot waiting to make
detailed notes on the back of an empty
cigarette packet. That's how near we all
were, had we but known it, Cask, to a global
holocaust of the first water. I shudder now
every time I think of it.

CASK: It's a sobering thought, sir, certainly.

HARKER: Fortunately, there weren't the atom secrets
around then that there are now, for me to
have on me. But I wasn't to know that at
the time.

CASK: Quite, sir.

HARKER: Since then, of course, it's happened to me
more times than I'd care to count, but
except for the occasional lapse, I flatter
myself I've managed by and large to keep
it under control. You learn over the years,
Cask, to take precautions.

CASK: Yes, I imagine you do, sir.

HARKER: For one thing, I never venture out of this
office if I can help it without divesting my
mind of anything remotely top secret
before I go.

37

CASK: The wisest thing you could do, sir.

HARKER: And I might say, Cask, without wishing to sound in any way smug, that even when I'm here I know considerably less about what goes on in my own department than almost any other Head of Security this side of Western Australia.

CASK: I don't think anyone would deny that, sir.

HARKER: And it's as it should be, Cask. A man can hardly expect to have much success in keeping vital secrets from other people if he isn't capable of keeping them from himself.

CASK. No, sir.

HARKER: That's a point worth remembering, Cask, if you're ever in my shoes.

CASK: Yes—I'll bear it in mind, sir.

HARKER: What were we talking about?

CASK: The leaked information, sir, on Operation Sturgeon Roe.

HARKER: Ah, yes.

CASK: What I've done so far is to try and contain the thing by denying that there's anything to it.

HARKER: Excellent plan.

CASK: And I thought—as I believe we said—that the Fawcetts should be kept under strict surveillance.

HARKER: Absolutely. Who have we got?

CASK: We decided, if you remember, sir, to put Andreyevsky Bolsover Griffiths on to it.

HARKER: Splendid. First class man.

CASK: Brief him to recover the capsule at the same time, perhaps.

HARKER: If you think it's feasible, Cask. By all means.

38

CASK : Without arousing their suspicions, of
course.
HARKER : Fine. Whatever you think, Cask.
CASK : I thought we might infiltrate him as Head
Porter . . .
HARKER : Yes.
CASK : . . . in the block of flats where they live.
HARKER : Yes. Well—deal with it as you think fit,
Cask. I leave it entirely with you.
He goes out into his office.

ACT ONE

SCENE 5

The Fawcetts' living-room. Evening. Next day.
*On the table is some torn brown paper wrapping which
was round the application form when it came. It in fact
consists of a sheaf of papers nearly two inches thick, with
which* LEONARD *is struggling on the table for several minutes
before* LILIAN *comes in.*

LILIAN : Application form indeed. I don't know
what you could have been thinking of.
Pause.
The very thing I said not to do. Before you
went to the phone. Not to get yourself
involved.
Pause. LILIAN *takes up her knitting and*
LEONARD *surveys the task ahead of him.*
I suppose we ought to be thankful they're
not asking for it in triplicate.
Pause. LEONARD *sits at the desk. Picks up a*

pen and tries to decide where to begin.
I can't think what possessed you.
Pause.
I don't suppose you even put a cross for no
publicity.
Pause.
Did you?

LEONARD : There was nowhere to *put* a cross, Lilian.
It was done on the phone.
Pause.

LILIAN : If they needed us, they'd get in touch with
us. We don't have to go out of our way.
Pause.

LEONARD : There are one or two things going on,
Lilian, that could do with looking into
from the inside, that's all.
Pause.

LILIAN : What do they want to know?

LEONARD : They want to know my antecedents.
Pause.

LILIAN : What I can't understand is where you got
the idea from that *I'd* want to be included
on it.

LEONARD : I just asked him. While I was about it.
That's all. We're neither of us committed.
It was just an ordinary routine enquiry
while I happened to be on the phone
talking to him.
Pause.

LILIAN : If *you* want to do it, for the sake of an
outside interest, that's up to you. But
they're not getting me up to my neck in
mud on some assault course or other . . .

LEONARD : I doubt whether it's that kind of training,
Lilian.

LILIAN: . . . and I shouldn't have thought *you* were
exactly cut out for it, either.
Pause.
In any case, if it's true what they say in
the paper, about automation, you're going
to be redundant before you get in.
Pause.
I wondered what it was you were on
tenterhooks for. Every time the post came.

LEONARD: I wasn't on tenter-hooks for it, Lilian. I
was just wondering when they were going
to send it.
Long pause as LILIAN *knits and* LEONARD
*works his way to the bottom of page one and
turns over.*

LEONARD: (*quoting*). "Have you ever suffered from
secret fears, inner tensions, inherited
grudge, deep-seated lack of confidence,
etc."
Pause.

LILIAN: You'll have to try and think of something.
It shouldn't be difficult.

LEONARD: (*quoting*). "Have you, or has any member
of your family, any history of failure? If so,
please give details."

LILIAN: They'd naturally want to know all that.
That's exactly what I should have expected
them to want to know. I could have told
you that before you sent for it.
Pause.
They're bound to be looking to see where
the chinks are in your armour.

LEONARD: What armour?

LILIAN: So that they can have something to probe
through. If they want to break you down

LEONARD : History of failure. . . .

Pause.

LILIAN : What about the half share you had in that refuse tip that went bankrupt? You could put that in.

Pause.

And there's the time you took up boxing.

LEONARD : Yes. I've thought of that.

Pause.

LILIAN : When you had six months with one of the leading boxing coaches in the country.

LEONARD : He wasn't a *leading* boxing coach, Lilian.

Pause.

LILIAN : And walked out of the gym on the very last day straight into the arms of that all-in wrestler.

Pause. LILIAN *glances out of the window and nods to someone.*

And got thrown from one side of Camberwell High Street to the other. Or wherever it was. That could go down.

Pause. LEONARD *starts reluctantly writing.*

And there's that dream you had. You ought to mention that.

Pause.

Where they ask about deep-seated lack of confidence.

LEONARD : I don't know which dream you're referring to, Lilian.

LILIAN : When you were thinking about taking up ladies' hairdressing. Don't you remember? And you had a dream about opening up one morning, only to find that the entire female population had gone bald overnight.

42

Pause.
That's the kind of thing they're looking
for, isn't it?

LEONARD: Yes.
Pause.

LILIAN: I should put it down then.

LEONARD *happens to look out of the window
and then looks again. He puts his pen down,
gets up, sidles round towards the window,
and standing well back and to one side, peers
out. Then he goes back to the desk and sits
down again.*

He's got to find his way around. It's only
his second day here.

LEONARD: He's not finding his way around by
hanging about out there, Lilian.
Pause.

LILIAN: Only last week you were saying, "Isn't it
time we had a head porter in the block."
Now we've got one, all you do is stare out
of the window at him. Every time he puts
in an appearance.
Pause.
What sort of an impression he'll get I can't
imagine.
Pause.
If he were taking all that much interest in
us, he'd hardly put on a head porter's
uniform to do it in, would he?

LEONARD: That may be how you look at it, Lilian.
Pause.
I prefer to think he's been sent here.

LILIAN: With a name like Briggs?

LEONARD: He wasn't sent here with a name like Briggs,
Lilian. He took that when he got here.

43

Pause.

This is the way they get at you.

LILIAN: So you keep saying.

Pause.

LEONARD: You've only got to look at his uniform.

Pause. ·

Frock coat and striped trousers. Have *you* ever seen the head porter of a block of flats wearing a frock coat and striped trousers?

There is a knock at the door which leads into the hall, and ANDREYEVSKY *appears at it. He should be perfectly recognizable beneath the heavy disguise. He is got up to look like the stage stereotype of the forelock-touching faithful retainer, in shabby frock coat and striped trousers. He is in* LILIAN'S *line of vision but not* LEONARD'S.

LILIAN: Yes, Briggs?

ANDREYEVSKY: Begging your pardon, ma'am. Begging your pardon, sir. It's the overflow. From the cistern, sir.

LILIAN: Yes. By all means, Briggs. You know the way. Second door on the left.

ANDREYEVSKY: Thank you, ma'am. Thank you, sir.

He shuffles and goes out into the back.

Pause.

LEONARD: What in God's name were you thinking about, Lilian? Sending him out there. It's exactly what he was after. It's playing right into his hands.

LILIAN: I don't know what you're talking about, Leonard.

LEONARD: We happen to have a top secret capsule out there! That's what I'm talking about.

44

Pause.

The whole thing's a blind from beginning to end. I could see that yesterday the moment he announced himself. His whole get-up. And "begging your pardon, ma'am," and this business. (*Touching his forelock.*)

Pause.

LILIAN : I rather liked it.

LEONARD : But for heaven's sake, Lilian . . . !

LILIAN : I don't think there's anything wrong with civility.

LEONARD : But . . .

LILIAN : We're not exactly overburdened with it. Outside the house, or in.

Pause.

LEONARD : Can't you see, Lilian, that the whole . . . thing, is designed to pull the wool over our eyes? Lull us into thinking he's some faithful old retainer who's been in service here from time immemorial?

Pause.

Before we've had time to turn round he's given himself *carte blanch* to come poking about in our cistern whenever he feels like it.

Pause. LEONARD *tries to go back to his form.*

What's he doing? He's been there long enough to photograph everything in there ten times over.

LILIAN : He's doing his job, Leonard. That's all he's doing.

LEONARD *turns and notices that the cord supporting one of the pictures has gone.*

LEONARD : What's keeping that up?

45

LILIAN: What up?

LEONARD: The cord's disappeared.

They look at each other and at the picture.
LEONARD *approaches cautiously and tests it,*
but the picture seems fixed to the wall.
Pause.

LILIAN: Perhaps that's what he was doing
yesterday.

LEONARD: What who was doing?

LILIAN: When he said could he look under the
floorboards. He probably needed the cord.

LEONARD: Who did?

LILIAN: Briggs.

LEONARD: What was he doing under the floorboards
yesterday?

LILIAN: I didn't take much notice. An aerial
photograph of the room underneath, I
think.

Pause.

LEONARD: You know, don't you, Lilian, that there *is*
no room underneath?

LILIAN: He's the head porter, Leonard. Give him
the credit for knowing what he's doing.
Please!

Pause. He goes to the picture and tries it
again, but in vain. It won't budge.

He turns away from the picture, and as he
does so it begins to swing away from the
wall, on hinges, to reveal, set into the wall,
a panel covered with dials, switches,
lights and a large combination lock. It looks
like a very small replica of the door to a
bullion safe in the vaults of the Bank of
England. Both stare at it for a few moments.
Close it up before the dust gets in it.

LEONARD : But . . .

LILIAN : It's only a safe or something they've had put in. We shall know soon enough.

She replaces the picture.

In any case there's nothing we can do till we know the combination.

Pause.

LEONARD : That might be another six months, Lilian.

LILIAN : The longer it is before we know how to open it, the less likely we are to get involved with what's inside.

Pause.

Not that I can imagine it taking anybody else six months to find out.

LEONARD *has another look behind the picture.*

LILIAN : Leave it alone, Leonard, till you know what you're doing.

LEONARD *turns back to the application form.*

LEONARD : The sooner this is sent in, and I'm called up for interview, the better it'll be for all of us.

He sits, writes, and then is struck by a thought.

LEONARD : Yes. I think I might.

LILIAN : What?

LEONARD : I think I might do that.

Pause.

When he comes back in. See how he reacts.

Pause.

Here he comes now.

LILIAN : For heaven's sake don't get carried away. That's all I ask.

LEONARD : Ah, Briggs. Come in.

ANDREYEVSKY : Thank you, sir. Thank you, ma'am.

47

LEONARD : Everything all right now, is it?

ANDREYEVSKY : Yes, it is, sir. Thank you. It's all shipshape now, as you might say, sir.

LEONARD : Good. Tell me, Briggs. You're the head porter, I believe.

ANDREYEVSKY : That's right, sir.

LEONARD : Been here some time, have you?

ANDREYEVSKY : Oh yes, sir. I have.

LEONARD : I thought I'd seen you around.

ANDREYEVSKY : Twenty-five years all told, sir. Come Michaelmas.

LEONARD : As long as that?

ANDREYEVSKY : Give or take the odd two and a half decades.

LEONARD : We must see what we can do for you, Briggs.

ANDREYEVSKY : Thank you very much, sir.

LEONARD : In the meantime (*picking up the miniature grandfather clock and thrusting it bodily into* ANDREYEVSKY'S *arms*) a small token of our esteem and gratitude.

ANDREYEVSKY (*touching his forelock*). Thank you very much, sir. Thank you very much, ma'am.

LEONARD : You'll keep it under your hat. . . .

ANDREYEVSKY : Oh yes, sir.

LEONARD : We don't want half the British Isles round here, do we? Holding their hands out for grandfather clocks.

ANDREYEVSKY : You can rely on me, sir.

LEONARD : Once a thing like that gets about, before you know where you are you've got people queueing up outside the door and halfway down the stairs.

ANDREYEVSKY : Quite, sir.

LILIAN : Unless you happen to be living on the

48

ground floor.

ANDREYEVSKY : That's the one thing that might save you,
ma'am, if I might be permitted to say so.
(*As he goes to the door.*) I'll cherish this,
sir. Ma'am.

LEONARD : Yes. Do that. Any time you've got a spare
moment.

ANDREYEVSKY : Good night to you, sir. Good night to you,
ma'am.
He goes out.

LEONARD : Oh—and Briggs.

ANDREYEVSKY : (*off*). Yes, sir?

LEONARD : You might redecorate the walls on your
way out. There's a good chap.

ANDREYEVSKY : (*off*). Very good, sir. And thank you, sir.
Thank you very much.
LEONARD *goes masterfully back to the desk
and begins to write.* LILIAN *knits on in
eloquent silence. He manages to hold out for
some time, but not indefinitely.*

LEONARD : There's such a thing as meeting bluff with
bluff, Lilian.
Pause.
It's your wits against theirs in this game,
you know.
Pause.
There's a good deal more at stake here
than a grandfather clock.
Pause. LILIAN *gets up, very slowly and
deliberately, and goes to the upstage door.*

LILIAN : I'll get your Horlick's.
She goes out.

LEONARD : A good deal more.

END OF ACT ONE

ACT TWO

SCENE 1

The Office. Evening. Later. The miniature grandfather clock stands near the desk. HARKER, *who is sitting at the desk, has* LEONARD'S *application form open in front of him.* CASK *is standing beside him.*

It is some time before he speaks.

HARKER : Claims to have had two parents, I see.

CASK : That's right, sir.

HARKER : One father, one mother.

Pause.

HARKER : Seems as if *they* both had two, as well.

CASK : That's what he maintains, sir. Four grandparents.

HARKER : And eight great-grandparents, by the look of it.

CASK : Yes, sir.

Pause.

HARKER : The further you go back, the more people seem to have been involved. Eight, sixteen, thirty-two, sixty-four, a hundred and twenty-eight. Goes on doubling up indefinitely, as far as I can see.

CASK : We did work it out, actually, sir. On the computer.

HARKER : And what did you arrive at?

CASK : Well—the figure we were left with was somewhere in the region of eighteen million at the time of the Norman Conquest.

HARKER : Eighteen *million*? But that's completely
and utterly ridiculous, Cask. In 1066 the
entire population of the British Isles
couldn't have amounted to much more
than a million and a half. At the very
most.

CASK : That's rather how it struck *us*, sir, too.

HARKER : Just doesn't add up, does it?

CASK : It's just possible that the other sixteen
million or so were out of the country at
the time, sir.

HARKER : If they were, I'm not sure that it doesn't
raise more issues than it settles, Cask.

CASK : I know what you mean, sir.

HARKER : What possible reason could more than
sixteen million people have for being out
of the country just at that particular
time?

CASK : Quite, sir. When they were wanted for
Domesday Book, amongst other things.

HARKER : It would bear looking into, Cask. There's
not a word about it here, of course.
(*Leafing through*.) He seems to have kept
suspiciously quiet about the whole
business. Which would indicate that he's
got *something* to hide.

CASK : There is, I suppose, the remote possibility
that they were resident abroad.

HARKER : Sixteen million people, Cask? Resident
abroad? Takes a bit of swallowing,
doesn't it?

CASK : It's about the only explanation that seems
to fit the facts, sir.

HARKER : Well—all I can say is that if it's true,
Pause.

the whole thing takes on an even more
disquieting aspect than we'd bargained for.

CASK : Unless, of course, he's lying, sir.

HARKER : Any reason to suppose he is?

CASK : Only the inherent improbability behind the
story, sir.

HARKER : Yes. I see your point, Cask.

CASK : Eighteen million at the Norman Conquest
—what must it have been at the time of
Christ?

HARKER : Astronomical, I should think, Cask.
*He fetches up once more at the clock, and
fixes it with a sage stare in the hope of
drawing inspiration from it. Then he turns
away.*

CASK : Let alone the Garden of Eden.
HARKER *stops, stares in thought at the floor
for a moment, saunters to the tape machine,
absent-mindedly reads the message on it,
and then turns round to face* CASK, *leaning
against the wall behind him.*

HARKER : How many people do you understand
there to have *been* in the Garden of Eden,
Cask?

CASK : Well—just the two, sir. So far as I've
always understood.

HARKER : (*returning to the desk*). Yes. That's what *I*
thought.
He sits down at the file once again.

HARKER : (*closing the file*). Discrepancy somewhere.
*He gets up, crosses to the projector, and
switches it on. A picture of* LEONARD *is
thrown on to the screen.*

HARKER : Let's have another look at this rather
slippery gentleman.

52

They stare at the screen in silence for a long time.

HARKER: Who was it we were thinking he might be?

CASK: XB97438, sir.

Pause.

HARKER: XB97348 being . . . ?

CASK: XB97438, sir. He's the brains behind a vast international espionage network covering the whole civilized world, if you remember, sir.

There is another long silence. HARKER *goes up to the screen to scrutinize it more closely.*

HARKER: (*pointing at* LEONARD'S *left ear*). Looks like an ear.

CASK: That's how it struck the lab. people, too, sir.

HARKER: Yes. Well.

CASK: I don't know whether you'd care to look at *Mrs.* Fawcett, while we're here? We've got her in two rather nice poses.

HARKER: Where are they?

CASK: Here, sir.

HARKER: Right. Let's see them, then. For what it's worth.

CASK *projects a picture of* LILIAN.

Yes.

CASK *projects another identical picture of* LILIAN.

Let me see the first one again.

CASK *projects the first picture.*

Have we got anything on her?

CASK: Well—no, sir. Not unless she's a Mrs. J. R. Pluckmyrtle.

HARKER: And what have we got on *her*?

CASK *crosses to the card index on* HARKER'S *desk and flips through it.*

CASK: She's listed here, sir, somewhere.

HARKER *continues to stare at the screen.*

HARKER: I wonder if she could be some sort of decoy?

CASK: I don't honestly think so, sir, actually. (*With the card.*) Here we are, sir. Mrs. Jezebel Ruby Pluckmyrtle. Sardinia. 1929. Goatherd's moll.

HARKER: Yes. We've obviously got to play this very cool. Very cool indeed.

He goes through the motions of thinking on his feet.

HARKER: Avoid anything that might arouse undue suspicion. Keep them guessing for a day or two. Then—and only then—I think we might have one of them in for interview, Cask. That's how we'll play this one.

CASK: That's rather what we had in mind, if you remember, sir, when we sent the application form out.

HARKER: And quite right too, Cask. The sooner we get one of them officially on the strength, the sooner we can keep proper tabs on them.

CASK: Yes, sir.

HARKER: And another thing we'll do is to make use of the new girl. Hilda.

CASK: Gelda, sir.

HARKER: Excellent opportunity for her to prove herself, Cask.

CASK: Quite, sir.

HARKER: As well as giving us a hold over the Pluckmyrtles. A few good, unequivocal

54

pictures with hidden cameras while she's busy with him—and I think we might have this particular customer exactly where we want him, Cask.

CASK : Yes, sir.

HARKER : Not much we can do while he stays indoors, of course. But the moment he sets foot outside, we can start things moving. Have him tailed till he's clear of the house, slip him a "Lady Godiva At Home To Callers" Card, and await events.

CASK : Yes, sir. I'm sure you're right.

HARKER : Of course I'm right. It's the perfect answer.

He goes towards his room.

Put it in hand, Cask, will you?

CASK : Yes, sir.

HARKER *goes into his room, closes the door, and then opens it again.*

HARKER : Andreyevsky Bolsover Griffiths. What's he doing? He's the man for a job like this. Put him on to it.

CASK : Yes. I already have, sir.

HARKER : Excellent chap for an assignment of this nature.

CASK : Yes, sir. He is.

HARKER : First class man. Has he been briefed?

CASK : I briefed him myself, sir. Twenty-four hours ago.

HARKER : So he knows what he's up to then.

CASK : I'm quite sure he'll use every trick in the book, sir.

HARKER : Good. Let's hope he gets results, then.

HARKER *closes the door and* CASK *gathers up the file and goes out with it.*

ACT TWO

Scene 2

The living-room. Late evening. Later.

On LILIAN'S *chair, half unwrapped, is a parcel containing some two dozen black notebooks with pencils.*

A large box stands on the floor down centre. On it is written: The "Easi-Phit"—The Part-time Secret Service Special Agent's Home Disguise Kit. In it are false beards, eyebrows, wigs, glasses, hats, a yashmak outfit, and other items. LEONARD *is crouched in front of a mirror.*

LILIAN *comes in unnoticed by* LEONARD, *looks at him for a few moments, and then comes downstage to read the notice on the box.*

LILIAN : There's an art to that, you know.

LEONARD *spins round, startled, after having put on a sou'-wester. Under it he has on one false eyebrow, a pair of pince-nez, a false nose, and a yashmak. He is also wearing an armband on which is written: "Intelligence and Security Part-time Special".*

LEONARD : Precisely, Lilian. Precisely. It's precisely *because* there's an art to it that I'm getting my hand in.

LEONARD *snatches off the yashmak to reveal a black beard underneath.*

LILIAN : (*seeing the pile of notebooks*). And what's all this, then?

LEONARD *hastens to remove the notebooks to the desk, where he stacks them in neat piles.*

LEONARD : I'm just stocking up. There's no point in being caught unprepared. . . . I don't intend to use them all at once. . . . They're

56

bound to want to know what experience
I've had. In collecting information.

LILIAN: Where you think you're going to get
enough information from to fill up that
lot.

LEONARD: You don't need to go very far to get vital
information. Not if you look around for
it. And visit the right places.

LILIAN: London's underworld, I suppose.

LEONARD: Not necessarily. There are plenty of other
places. St. Paul's Cathedral, for instance. I
doubt whether the overall width of that has
ever been properly noted down in one of
those.

LILIAN: Or ever likely to be.

LEONARD: It's just a matter of getting my hand in,
Lilian. The last thing you want, if they ask
you to show your paces, is to let it be seen
that you're an absolute greenhorn.

LEONARD has removed everything except the
sou'-wester, which he has forgotten. He
goes towards the door into the hall.

LEONARD: The very last thing.

LILIAN: I can't see you looking any less like a
green horn *in* a sou'-wester than out of
one.

He takes it off.

LEONARD: Maybe not.

He goes out and comes back inside the door
with a third, very large, parcel.

All the same, you'll concede, I take it,
that there might be occasions when an
agent is called upon to make contact with
his opposite number in the pouring rain.

LEONARD goes out.

Pause. LILIAN *knits for a time in silence.*
Then she speaks towards the hall door,
where she thinks LEONARD *still is. We see*
him go past the open upstage door, with the
parcel.

LILIAN : I hope you're not going out somewhere.
At this time.
Pause.
Because if it's London's underworld you're
thinking of going out looking for, you'd
be better off leaving it to people who know
what they're doing.
Pause.
Somebody like you, hobnobbing with
crooks and gangsters. They'll see you
coming.
Pause.
It takes more than a sou'wester and a pair
of glasses to get yourself accepted in those
quarters.
Pause.
Leonard! Can you hear me?
She gets up to investigate.
I wish I'd never mentioned London's
underworld in the first place.
She looks into the hall and turns back
puzzled. As she does so, LEONARD *appears*
in the doorway at the back. He is wearing a
bear's skin, with the armband on, has an old
raincoat over his arm, and is carrying a grey
trilby hat.
(*after a pause*). I only hope that hasn't got
the moth in it.
Pause. LEONARD *goes to the door and out*
into the hall.

58

You're not intending to be seen out in it,
are you?

*LEONARD comes back in, without the hat
and raincoat, and starts getting out of the
skin. LILIAN helps him, by unzipping it.*

If you were going to a fancy dress ball,
there might be some point in it.

LEONARD : I was trying it on for size, Lilian. That's all.

LILIAN : What circles you expect a thing like that to
give you the entrée into, I can't imagine.

LEONARD : The bear happens to be the national
emblem of a rather large and not altogether
uninfluential country.

He steps out of the skin and is in his socks.

LILIAN : Get something on your feet, Leonard.
Please.

LEONARD : I'm just doing so.

He goes out to the back.

(*off*). Wear a thing like that in Moscow,
and you could go anywhere. If you played
your cards right.

*He comes back in, with his boots on, and
crosses to the other door.*

LEONARD : Straight into the Kremlin and no questions
asked.

He goes out.

LILIAN : I can just see you getting that kind of
assignment. As a part-time special.

*Pause. LEONARD, in the old raincoat and
grey trilby hat, comes in and stuffs his
pockets full of notebooks.*

LEONARD : Expect me in for breakfast.

He goes.

LILIAN : Why you need to be going out at all, I
can't for the life of me imagine.

LEONARD: (*off*). It's a matter of getting properly *au fait* with the *modus operandi*, Lilian. That's all. In readiness.

We hear the front door open and close.

LILIAN *starts tidying up the disguises.*

LILIAN: Mooching about from one sleazy haunt to another. Without so much as a street guide to show him his way around. And then wonders why his feet pay him out.

ACT TWO

SCENE 3

A Soho alleyway. Same.

LEONARD, *dressed exactly as when he left the house in the previous scene, has been cornered by* ANDREYEVSKY, *who has a suitcase full of large brown envelopes open on the ground, and is offering one to* LEONARD.

ANDREYEVSKY: A bargain, really. At the price. Hardly used.

LEONARD: Yes. Not a bad size, I suppose. Anybody wanting that size.

ANDREYEVSKY: Nice weight, too. Feel it—in your hand. Not too small, not too big.

LEONARD: Yes. I see what you mean.

ANDREYEVSKY: Sell a lot of those. Connoisseurs and people.

Pause.

One of the best sizes they bring out. In my opinion.

Pause.

Sold a treat in Ancient Greece that would have done.

60

LEONARD : It would?

ANDREYEVSKY : Oh, yes. Not too long, not too broad. They'd go for that. Classical, you see.

LEONARD : Ah.

ANDREYEVSKY : Like the Parthenon. Ever see the Parthenon?

LEONARD : No, I can't say I have.

ANDREYEVSKY : Beautiful size.

LEONARD : Yes?

ANDREYEVSKY : Not too long, not too broad. That's what does it, you see. Proportion. Length against width.

LEONARD : What are you asking for this? If it's not a rude question.

ANDREYEVSKY : Two guineas.

Pause.

They were hot on anything classical in those days of course.

LEONARD : Yes . . . I . . .

ANDREYEVSKY : Give them anything that wasn't classical and they wouldn't look at it.

Pause.

One of the things they're noted for. The Ancient Greeks. More than anything else.

Pause.

Tradition.

Pause.

That's why they'd have gone for that, of of course.

LEONARD : You think they would?

ANDREYEVSKY : Buff envelope that size? They'd have gone mad.

LEONARD : Really?

ANDREYEVSKY : They'd have been fighting in the streets for it.

LEONARD : Yes. Well . . .

ANDREYEVSKY : If I'd turned up in Athens with that envelope I'd have been mobbed.

LEONARD : I wonder. . . . Before I settle for it, I wonder if I could by any chance give it a trial?

ANDREYEVSKY : Do. By all means. Give it any trial you like.

LEONARD : Only I'd like to be absolutely sure before I take the plunge.

ANDREYEVSKY : Of course. Try it out. It's the only way. You won't tell otherwise.

LEONARD : No . . .

ANDREYEVSKY : Put it in the post. Hand it over the counter. Stand it behind the clock on the mantelpiece. See how it shapes up.

LEONARD : Thank you. I will.

ANDREYEVSKY : If you think you'd like it, come back and we'll clinch the deal.

LEONARD : That's very kind of you.

ANDREYEVSKY *takes a smaller white envelope from his pocket.*

ANDREYEVSKY : Oh—and here's a smaller envelope you can put inside if you want to. No charge for that. Present from the management.

LEONARD : Oh. (*Jocularly.*) Not a sprat to catch a mackerel, I trust.

ANDREYEVSKY : No, no. Just a token of goodwill. You don't have to give it back.

LEONARD : It's addressed to somebody. Does that matter? Ministry of Intelligence and Security.

ANDREYEVSKY : Oh, that's just . . . nothing. It's . . . (*he waves a hand*) . . . forget it.

LEONARD : Right. (*Getting up.*) And I'll be back when

I've tried this out, then.

ANDREYEVSKY : I hope you find it satisfactory.

ANDREYEVSKY closes his suitcase.

LEONARD : Are you coming my way?

ANDREYEVSKY : No. I've got one or two more calls to make.

LEONARD : See you in a week's time, then.

ANDREYEVSKY : Look forward to it. Good-bye.

LEONARD : Good-bye.

ANDREYEVSKY goes off. LEONARD stands looking round, then with a cautious glance over his shoulder, opens the envelope. He takes out the card inside, and reads it.
(*Reading from card*). Lady Godiva at home to callers by special invitation. Room 293 B. Any time. Day or night. Twenty-four hours' service.

GELDA appears in a white coat. She takes the card from him and leads him out.

GELDA : Room 293B? Do come in. I'll take you up in the lift.

They go off.

ACT TWO

SCENE 4

The Office. Same.
CASK is on the telephone, taking notes.

CASK : (*into 'phone*). Yes. . . . Yes. . . . Yes. . . .
Yes. . . . Do I understand, Mrs. . . . (*He hunts for the name on a piece of paper.*)
Crouchleaper, that you have evidence that they were landed at Scarborough by

63

submarine? . . . Not at all, it's simply . . .
Yes. It's simply that it's unusual for this to
happen. . . . Good heavens, no, Mrs.
Crouchleaper. I'm not doubting your word
at all. . . . We certainly will look into it.
. . . Oh, yes. . . . You did right to let us
know. . . . We will. . . . Most certainly we
will. . . . Yes. Absolutely the right thing. . . .
We're very grateful that you were public-
spirited enough to . . . Yes, indeed, Mrs.
Crouchleaper. . . . And thank you for . . .
Yes. Good-bye, Mrs. . . . Indeed we will.
. . . Good-bye, Mrs. Crouchleaper.
HARKER *has come in towards the end of the
conversation.*

CASK : (*to* HARKER). Sixteen ostriches landed by
submarine on the east coast near
Scarborough. Sounds a bit unlikely,
doesn't it, sir?

HARKER : What have we got up there?

CASK : Nothing that we've so far been able to
track down, sir.

HARKER : East coast near Scarborough. Isn't that
where the trawlers are hanging about?
Offshore?

CASK : That's right, sir. And there's also that
group of Cossacks we located on the moors
up there. With five pairs of binoculars
between three of them. We never pinned
down what *they* were after, either.

HARKER : Isn't there a riding school up there?

CASK : There are several, sir.

HARKER : Cossacks. Riding schools. There's a
connection there, Cask. Somewhere.

CASK : We rather dismissed that idea, sir, if you

remember.

HARKER : What idea?

CASK : That the Cossacks might be taking too much interest in our horsemanship training methods, sir. We decided it was rather too obvious a blind, sir.

HARKER : Get us all legging it up as fast as we can to Scarborough, so that they can send somebody shinning up Nelson's Column with a notebook and tape-measure while our backs are turned.

CASK : Roughly that, sir.

HARKER : Yes. Must be *some*thing up there. Cask. Otherwise, why Scarborough every time?

CASK : We've combed the area, sir, for clues as to what it might be that they know about and we as yet don't—but you know what it's like with these Class One Special Priority Emergency Rainbow Top Secret projects, sir.

HARKER : If enemy intelligence can find out what they are, Cask, I should have thought it was incumbent on us to put up some sort of a show ourselves in the same direction.

CASK : We've got as many of our best people up there as we can spare, sir.

HARKER : I mean, we know all about Rule 93B. But Rule 93B was never meant to be a cloak for genuine incompetence. And in any case it's amply catered for already by questions in the House, fulminations in the Press, Royal Commissions, spy trials, and I don't know what else. The fact is, Cask, that in this country we have the finest apparatus for hoodwinking the enemy that exists anywhere in the world.

CASK: I'm sure we have, sir.

HARKER: And I think we can say we've made full and effective use of it to create an image we can be justly proud of. As a bunch of bumblingly incompetent old women.

CASK: Yes, sir.

HARKER: It's an image which is of incalculable value, Cask. Behind which the real work can go on unhampered. And it's one which we must do all in our power to preserve.

CASK: Quite, sir.

HARKER: Short, however, of actually living up to it. Which we're in grave danger of doing over this Scarborough business, Cask.

CASK: That's very true, sir.

HARKER: Trawlers, Cossacks, ostriches. It must tie up somehow, Cask. If we address ourselves to the problem.

CASK: It's difficult to know where to start, really, sir.

HARKER: This woman, for instance. Do we know who she is?

CASK: Mrs. Crouchleaper? She's, as far as I know, sir, a local housewife.

HARKER: I mean, are we reasonably certain that she isn't someone totally different, who happens to have the same name?

CASK: Well, sir . . .

HARKER: That's the kind of possibility that all too easily gets overlooked.

CASK: I don't in this case, sir . . .

HARKER: Or for that matter have you explored the other possibility that the ostriches she's claiming to have seen were in fact kidnapped by a gang of wild-life

66

HARKER : enthusiasts and dumped there on orders from an unnamed foreign power?

CASK : Well . . .

HARKER : Or simply because the trail was getting too hot.

CASK : They did specifically have their heads in the sand, sir, on the three separate occasions she saw them.

HARKER : And where does that get us?

CASK : I think it's a pretty fair inference, sir, that they were on the look-out for subversive underground activities.

HARKER : Do you think they were?

CASK : It's at least on the cards, sir.

HARKER : Yes. I almost hope you're right, Cask. One gets a little jittery at times. At what one might have unwittingly laid oneself open to, in an unguarded moment.

CASK : In the way of investigation, sir?

HARKER : By one's own side, Cask, yes.

CASK : I doubt, sir, whether they'd send ostriches all the way to Scarborough by submarine, in order to check on the movements of the Head of Security in London. It doesn't make sense.

HARKER : Strange things can happen, Cask. Strange things can happen. One's had similar experiences too often, not to get a little apprehensive.

CASK : All the same, sir . . .

HARKER : Hard sometimes not to lose faith, Cask. Faith in oneself, faith in what one's doing.

CASK : Perhaps it's as well not to dwell too much on it, sir.

HARKER : In fact there's a great temptation, sometimes, to put an end once and for all to the struggle.

CASK : You mean . . . ?

HARKER : Simply denounce oneself publicly as a security risk, Cask.

CASK : I don't think, sir . . .

HARKER : Which, let's face it, Cask, I am.

CASK : That's perfectly true, sir, but . . .

HARKER : I know, Cask. I know what you're going to say. Nothing worse for undermining public confidence.

CASK : The whole fabric would crumble under us!

HARKER : Yes. It's the one thing that keeps my lips sealed. The thought of the repercussions it could have.

CASK : I think they'd be rather widespread, sir.

HARKER : Rather touching, Cask, isn't it? The faith people have in one.

CASK'S *'phone rings. He picks it up.*

CASK : It is, sir. (*Into 'phone.*) Yes? . . . Oh. Right. Thank you. (*He puts the 'phone down. To* HARKER.) The Press, sir. They're waiting for us downstairs now.

HARKER *looks bemused.*

CASK : We promised them a statement, sir. If you remember. On the new policy line.

HARKER : We did?

CASK : I've got it here, sir, if you want to refresh your memory.

HARKER : Let me see.

CASK *hands a typed sheet to* HARKER.

(*reading*). "As a gesture of confidence in the economic system which we on this side of the iron curtain are pledged to defend, it is proposed that the whole of our

68

intelligence and security services be
handed over to private enterprise." Yes.

HARKER *and* CASK *go out into the corridor,
as* GELDA *and* LEONARD *come in through the
other door.* GELDA *has a long white coat,
and goes to a shelf for a form.*

GELDA: I'm sorry about this, Mr. Fawcett. But we
have to do it, in order to satisfy the powers
that be. They make a lot of fuss if we don't.
It's just to say you're quite satisfied with
the way it's gone.

LEONARD: Yes. Of course.

GELDA: If you could sign there and there.

LEONARD: (*signing*). Here?

GELDA: And there.

LEONARD: Well, thank you very much, Miss . . .

GELDA: Gelda. It's what I'm known as while I'm
duty.

LEONARD: . . . Gelda. For your very welcome
ministrations. It's . . . a very great relief.

LEONARD *throughout behaves with what he
imagines to be old-world courtesy, mingling
with it a stiffly waggish gallantry, none of
which ever begins to come off.* GELDA *is at
first trying gently to get him out, but then
gives up and lets him go on, slightly playing up
to him, amused and curious and sympathetic.*

GELDA: I'm glad.

LEONARD: You've been most expert.

GELDA: Oh . . .

LEONARD: Skilful handling. It makes all the
difference. I'm very grateful.

GELDA: It was nothing, really.

LEONARD: On the contrary. You've been a great help.
A very great help. I don't know what I

69

should have done without you.

GELDA: It's nice of you to say so, but . . .

LEONARD: No. It's true. I'm very greatly indebted to you.

GELDA: It was nothing at all. Really.

LEONARD: Oh, yes. You're being far too modest about it.

GELDA: Me? Goodness. I'd never thought of myself as being modest, I must say.

LEONARD: Far too modest.

GELDA: The very last thing I should have said about myself.

LEONARD: The most modest woman I've ever had the pleasure of meeting. By far.

GELDA: Well—it's very flattering to be told so, but it isn't true, I'm afraid. I only wish it were.

LEONARD: You're too modest about it.

GELDA: Am I?

LEONARD: You should be proud of your modesty.

GELDA: Oh—I don't . . .

LEONARD: You play yourself down too much.

GELDA: Perhaps I do. It's just that I'm not very good at singing my own praises, I suppose.

LEONARD: Nonsense. You could sing them as well as anyone else if you tried.

GELDA: You think so?

LEONARD: Better, probably, than a good many of them.

GELDA: You may be right. It's just that I've never looked on myself as being a particularly boastful sort of person, that's all.

LEONARD: You? Not a boastful person?

GELDA: Good heavens, no.

LEONARD: Come now.

GELDA: I'm just about as modest as anyone could be.

70

LEONARD : *Modest?*

GELDA : Terribly modest. It's a . . . joke with people. I'm just about as far at the other end of the scale from being boastful as you could possibly get.

LEONARD : Well—all I can say is that appearances are very deceptive.

GELDA : They often are, aren't they?

LEONARD : I should have backed you against practically anybody.

GELDA : No. Not me.

LEONARD : (*wagging a finger*). Are you sure you're not being unduly modest?

GELDA : No. It's perfectly true. Really. You can ask anyone. They'll all say the same. It's the thing everybody notices about me when they first meet me.

LEONARD : (*patting the back of her hand*). I think you're just being unduly modest.

GELDA : Well . . .

LEONARD : And I'm sticking to my opinion, too.

GELDA : If you insist, Mr. Fawcett.

LEONARD : Leonard is the . . .

GELDA : Would you like me to book an appointment for you for next month?

LEONARD : Er . . . yes, please.

GELDA : At the same time on the eighteenth?

LEONARD : That would be excellent. Thank you.

GELDA : And meanwhile, if you could try to throw more of your weight on to the *ball* of your foot, Mr. Fawcett, when walking, rather than on the extreme outside edge of the small toe, as you're doing at present, I think you'll find it will help to keep the tendons from getting overstretched, as

71

well as avoiding a recurrence of the blisters.

LEONARD: Oh. Yes. Right. I'll do that.

GELDA: And next time, as well as the two corns on the big toe, we'll see whether we can do anything to tone up the muscles of the heel and instep.

LEONARD: Thank you. Thank you very much.

GELDA: Good-bye, then, Mr. Fawcett.

LEONARD: Good-bye...Gelda. And...very grateful....

GELDA: Not at all.

She finally manages to close the door on LEONARD, *stands for a moment or two collecting herself together, and then with a shrug crosses briskly and out into the adjoining office.*

ACT TWO

SCENE 5

The Fawcetts' living-room. Morning. Next day.

The telephone has been moved from the hall to the living-room. On the mantelpiece is an envelope similar to the one that ANDREYEVSKY *foisted on to* LEONARD, *except that it is overprinted in red with the words:* "*Top Secret. Photographs with Care.*"

LEONARD *is sitting at the breakfast table.* LILIAN, *who has finished her own breakfast, comes in with a boiled egg for* LEONARD.

LILIAN: All night long, heaven only knows where.

She puts the egg down in front of him.

(*Going out again.*) And you're not a whit

72

the wiser for it.

LEONARD: It isn't a question of that, Lilian. As I keep
telling you, you pick up the atmosphere.
Pause.

LILIAN: (*returning*). I should hardly have thought it
was worth staying out all night for.

LEONARD: It is if there's something to be gained from
it.

LILIAN *sits and picks up the paper.*

LILIAN: As long as you feel you have.
Pause.

LEONARD: There's no substitute for being on the spot
when things are happening. It's one of the
first rules you have to learn in this game.
Pause.

LILIAN: And what did happen?

LEONARD: Last night? Nothing. In particular. As it
turned out.
Pause.

Apart from the general ambience.
Pause.

LILIAN: Soho, I suppose.

LEONARD: Round there, yes. That area.
Pause.

LILIAN: Not exactly the most salubrious of
neighbourhoods. I must say. To spend the
small hours in.
Pause.

Isn't that where all the sleazy haunts are?

LEONARD: There's . . . one or two, yes.

LILIAN: I thought so.
Pause.

Trudging round from one to another all
night.

LEONARD *has a momentary spasm of alarm,*

73

but it goes when he sees LILIAN *continue reading*.

Just so that you can tell them you've done a tour of duty somewhere in London's West End.

Pause.

What on earth you were expecting to find. At that hour. In pitch darkness.

Pause.

If it was the strange, twilight world of London's crooks and gangsters you were looking for, I should have thought you'd have been better off doing it in daylight.

LEONARD: They don't operate in daylight, Lilian.

Pause.

LILIAN: So it *was* the strange, twilight world of crooks and gangsters you were out looking for, then.

LEONARD: I was . . . keeping my eyes open, yes.

LILIAN: I thought that's what you'd been up to.

Pause.

LILIAN: If I'd known that's what you were going to do, I could have told you in advance to leave it till there was enough light to see by.

LEONARD: Yes—and defeat the whole purpose of the operation. I keep trying to explain to you, Lilian. It's got to be done under cover of darkness.

LILIAN: I don't see why.

LEONARD: Because it so happens, Lilian, that it's under cover of darkness that the grim and sinister drama of international espionage is played out! That's all.

Pause.

I'm not responsible for it. It just happens

74

like that.
Pause.

LILIAN: We know it does, Leonard. We know they play out the grim and sinister drama of international espionage under cover of darkness.

LEONARD: Well, then.

LILIAN: And always have done. . . . *When* it suits them to.
Pause.

They don't play it out every single night of the year. Wet or fine. Just to please any chance visitor who might happen to stray in and wants to see them at it.
Pause.

LEONARD: For any chance visitor, Lilian, maybe not.
Pause.

LILIAN: And I can't see them making a special point of playing it out there and then, the moment you put your nose inside the door, just because you happen to have an armband in your pocket, with *Intelligence and Security* written on it.
Pause.

It's a complete waste of a good night's sleep.
They both lapse into silence, as LILIAN *reads and* LEONARD *eats.*

LEONARD: (*looking at* LILIAN's *paper as she reads*).
Someone else laid himself open, I see.
Pause.

(*reading from the paper*). "On the basis of photographs taken with a hidden camera."
What's *he* been up to, then?

LILIAN: I don't know. I haven't got to it yet.

Pause.

LEONARD : Compromising situation, I suppose. Of
some sort. Why *do* they do it?

Pause.

The oldest trick in the book. Plays right
into their hands.

*Pause. He finishes his breakfast and gets
up.*

All they've got to do is get a picture of him
in the act, whatever it is, threaten to leak
it to the Press, and they've got him.
Nobody wants to see a picture of himself
splashed all over the front of the paper
with his socks off having his corns . . .

LILIAN : Leonard! Please!

LEONARD *has in any case stopped short, on
seeing the envelope on the mantelpiece for
the first time. He seems transfixed by it.*
LILIAN *gives him a sharp look.*

LILIAN : In any case, how did you know it was a
chiropodist he'd been visiting?

LEONARD : Oh. Was it? I didn't know. It just . . . I
mean it often is. . . . You know what
people are like about their . . . feet.

LILIAN : Yes, Leonard. All right. You don't have to
go on about it.

Pause.

LEONARD : (*elaborately casual*). Who is it? Some
embassy official, I expect.

Pause.

Do they say?

LILIAN : I'm just looking.

Pause.

No. They don't seem to give a name. Just
"a man" . . . "seen visiting a chiropodist"

... "late yesterday evening".

LEONARD *relaxes and edges nearer the envelope.*

They'll probably give his name in a later edition.

LEONARD *stops dead in his tracks and then continues.*

LEONARD : We . . . don't know what he was going there for, of course.

LILIAN : He certainly wasn't going there to play halma, Leonard. That we do know.

Pause.

And whatever it was we can be pretty certain he was paying out a small fortune for the privilege.

Pause.

LEONARD : It's always possible he was taken short, I suppose.

LILIAN : Taken short?

LEONARD : He could have been.

LILIAN : Really!

Pause.

What with? Bunions?

She puts the paper down, gets up and begins to clear the table.

Anybody would think he was a friend of yours. The way you try to defend him.

LILIAN *goes out with plates and* LEONARD *seizes the opportunity to take the envelope and look at it. He is caught with it in his hand when* LILIAN *comes back in.*

Oh, yes. Somebody called. During the night. Did I know where you were and would I give you that?

LILIAN *gathers up some things and goes to*

77

the door with them.

"Photographs with Care," or something.
She stops for a second, as the thing connects up for the first time in her mind, and then goes on out.

LEONARD *opens the envelope, convinced of the worst, and pulls out several photographs. They are large, glossy prints, showing him with* GELDA *and including embarrassing close-ups of his bare feet. He looks at them in horror and then panics. He stuffs them back in the envelope, rushes to the safe, fiddles ineffectually with the lock, looks frantically round for some other hiding place, and in the end slips them under the curled up corner of the carpet, as* LILIAN *comes back in with an empty tray.*

LEONARD : (*getting up*). It's time I got this tacked down, Lilian. It's . . . We're going to have an accident with it if I don't do it soon. I'll get a hammer. And a few tacks.
He goes. LILIAN *looks after him, then looks at the mantelpiece, then at the carpet. She goes to where the envelope is, takes it out, looks inside, and registers a sort of horrified satisfaction. She puts the contents back in the envelope, takes it very deliberately across the room, places it on his desk, and goes back to finish clearing the table.*
LEONARD *comes back with a hammer and tacks, and without looking at* LILIAN *begins tacking the carpet down.*

LEONARD : Get it done now, and it's done. Otherwise I shall keep putting it off and putting it off, and it'll never get done.

LILIAN *lets him get the very last tack*
hammered home before she says a word.
There. I think that should do the trick.
LILIAN *picks up the tray.*

LILIAN: I've put the envelope with the pictures in
it over there. On your desk.

LEONARD: What? What pictures? Those are not . . .
Which ones?
LILIAN *withers him with a stare.*

LILIAN: (*breaking and going out*). At your age. I
hardly know whether to laugh or cry.
Pause. LILIAN *comes back in.*

LEONARD: How do we know this isn't a forgery?

LILIAN: If it is, it's been done by an expert.
Pause.

LEONARD: What else did . . . they want?

LILIAN: Nothing. Give you that, and did I think
you were a fit and proper person.
Pause.
They weren't in here for more than a
minute.

LEONARD: They?

LILIAN: Him.
Pause.

LEONARD: You mean . . . in here?

LILIAN: Where else?

LEONARD: But what doing?

LILIAN: Looking round, I suppose. Taking
stock.
Pause.
Something about recognizing the place
again if it ever arose.

LEONARD: If what ever arose?

LILIAN: They didn't say.
LILIAN *goes out to the back. She returns to*

*fetch something and checks in the doorway
as she goes out again.*

A whole grandfather clock squandered—
with nothing to show for it but a wall safe
we don't even know how to open. And
now—chiropody!

She goes out. The front doorbell rings.
(*Off.*) I'll go.

LILIAN *comes in and is crossing to the other
door when the telephone rings. She checks,
is for a moment in two minds whether
to go to the door or answer the telephone,
and then, as the doorbell rings a second
time, abandons the telephone to* LEONARD.

For heaven's sake, don't get us involved in
anything else. (*Going out.*) Have the sense
for once to say you're the South Western
Gas Board.

LEONARD : (*into 'phone*). United Dairies.

*His face slowly subsides into dumbfounded
incredulity.*

(*Into 'phone.*) . . . Right . . . (*He lowers the
'phone, dazedly, then raises it again.*)
. . . Thank you.

*He puts it down and stares in front of him
like a man concussed.*

Sixteen pints till further notice at the
Moldavian Embassy.

He continues to stand there motionless, as
LILIAN *comes back in, opening a letter.*

LILIAN : For you. By special messenger.

She reads the letter and hands it to LEONARD.
The Selection Board.

LEONARD : What? Oh.

LILIAN : They're seeing you next week.

*She stands looking at him for a moment as
he stares down, unseeing, at the letter in his
hand, and then goes to the door at the back.*

ACT TWO

SCENE 6

The Office. Evening. Later.
HARKER *and* CASK *deep in thought.*

HARKER : So one would assume that the Cossacks
are to divert attention from the ostriches,
while the trawlers are diverting attention
from the Cossacks.

CASK : That would seem to add up, sir.

HARKER : Yes. On the other hand it doesn't get us
very much further.

CASK : File 879 BZQ, sir. (*He goes for the file.*)
This may tie up. Why didn't I think of this
before?

HARKER *pauses in front of the grandfather
clock.*

HARKER : I feel sure the key to it all is in this room,
somewhere, Cask.

CASK : (*with file*). I think you may well be right, sir.

HARKER : I keep getting drawn back for some reason
to this, Cask. That's where we shall find
the answer. In there. You mark my words.

CASK : (*showing* HARKER *the file*). Here it is, sir. I
knew I'd seen this somewhere. It's just
connected. Do you see that, sir? Difficult
to make out, but unmistakably . . .

HARKER : Yes. Yes. You may well have stumbled on

to something here, Cask. We'll have a
look at this.

HARKER *takes a picture from the file to the
projector.*

Confirm it one way or the other, and see
what else we can make out as well.

*A picture is thrown on to the screen of an
ostrich. It is looking round into the camera,
its head having apparently been lifted out of
the sand for the purpose, one eye being
enormously enlarged behind a monocle.*

*From the rear of the ostrich trails a length
of cable which disappears into a junction box.*

HARKER: A telescopic monocle, by heaven!

CASK: And wired for vision. Or sound.

HARKER: Or more likely both.

CASK: So now we know what the trawlers are doing.

HARKER: Picking it up and relaying it back as fast
as it comes in. The whole thing's beginning
to make sense at last.

CASK: All too much sense, sir.

HARKER: A brilliant stroke, Cask.

CASK: I knew I'd seen this somewhere, sir, but
for the moment I couldn't quite remember
in what connection. And then it came back
to me that we'd had these pictures
smuggled out from their Zoological
Warfare Special Intelligence Training
Centre in Upper Siberia.

HARKER: We obviously didn't pay nearly enough
attention to them at the time, Cask.

CASK: That's very true. We didn't, sir.

HARKER: It was a mistake, Cask.

CASK: It was indeed, sir.

HARKER: A very grave mistake.

CASK : I don't think we came within a mile of realizing just how far they'd advanced in this field, sir.

HARKER : We do now, Cask.

CASK : To have a secret service weapon as sophisticated as this not only in production but actually in operation in so short a time suggests that they're really going in for this in a big way.

HARKER : Makes the carrier pelican of a few years back completely and utterly obsolete at one stroke.

CASK : We really thought we were on to something there, sir. Didn't we?

HARKER : Always a vulnerable weapon, Cask. It sounds impressive—the flying diplomatic bag. But in practice. . . . Pouch bulging with top secret documents—somebody throws the thing a sardine and we've lost the lot.

CASK : It leaves us very little to counter this with, sir.

HARKER : We've got nothing, Cask. That's the truth of it. Not a thing to touch it.

CASK : Unless you can count the caterpillars.

HARKER : Hardly a match for this kind of thing, Cask.

CASK : I suppose not, sir.

HARKER : Training caterpillars to eat coded messages into cabbage leaves? If that's the best we can do, we may as well opt out altogether.

CASK : True enough, sir.

HARKER : So. That's the ostriches accounted for. It still doesn't get us very much further with the Cossacks, though.

HARKER, *deep in thought, walks round the*

83

room and fetches up at the grandfather clock.
This is where the answer is, I feel sure of
it. In some way. This is what one keeps
coming back to.

CASK : Should we open up the front and look
inside, sir?

HARKER : Yes. Do that, Cask.

*CASK opens the door at the front of the
clock. On a bar running across the inside of
the door a tie is hanging. It is a white tie
with small black spots.* HARKER *takes it off
and looks at it.*

Here it is, Cask. Under our eyes the whole
time. As always happens. Why didn't we
do this weeks ago?

CASK : Microdots!

HARKER *takes the microdot off the tie,
places it on a slide, and examines it through
a magnifying glass.*

HARKER : Yes. That looks very promising.
*He inserts the slide in the projector and
switches on. We see a picture in close-up of
a string bag full of groceries.*

CASK : Prototype LKJR Mark XVI, by God!

HARKER : Yes, Cask. The only string bag in the whole
wide world with a false bottom—and now
as good as on the scrapheap. Years of
research gone for nothing. (*He switches off.*)

CASK : What do you think's behind it, sir?

HARKER : Let's piece it together. He wears the tie.
He goes to Scarborough. Perhaps on a day
trip—engineered for the purpose. Once
there—what can he do? One of two things.
He can go walking on the moors, or he
can go walking along the front. Let us say

84

he chooses the moors. In that case . . .

HARKER *moves towards the projector.*

. . . the Cossacks will have five pairs of long-range binoculars trained on . . .

He switches on the projector. We see on the screen the string bag as before.

On the other hand, he may decide to take a stroll near the beach. In that case, sixteen ostriches—each one equipped with a powerful telescopic monocle—are going to whip their heads out of the sand the moment he comes within range, and within seconds every radar screen from one end to the other of an unnamed foreign power will have a picture on it as large as you like of a project that it's taken us nineteen years to bring to completion. That's the situation here, Cask, as I see it.

HARKER *switches off.*

CASK : It certainly seems to add up, sir.

HARKER : What it amounts to, Cask, is that we've stumbled on to something a good deal bigger than we initially imagined.

CASK : It does begin to look like it, sir.

HARKER : Something that could have shattering consequences of a pretty far-reaching kind, Cask.

CASK : Well . . .

HARKER : For which I would have no alternative but to hold myself personally responsible.

CASK : Unless we can nip the whole thing in the bud, sir.

HARKER : A betrayal of trust. That's how it would be interpreted, Cask. By one's fellow countrymen. If ever it got out that one had

been responsible—however indirectly—for
a situation of this kind.

CASK: That's true, sir, but . . .

HARKER: It's a desperate situation to find oneself
in, Cask. Desperate.

CASK: Why don't we have him abducted, sir?
When he comes up for interview. Before
the Selection Board. Next Tuesday.

HARKER: No, Cask. There's only one thing that can
save us. And that's decisive action now.
Next week may be too late.

CASK: But don't you think, sir . . . ?

HARKER: No, Cask. We can't afford the luxury of
acting through the usual channels. There's
too much at stake. We've got to act now.
With complete ruthlessness if necessary.
Ruthlessness and subterfuge.
It's all we can do.

CASK: But . . .

HARKER: We're fighting a war of nerves, Cask. It's
no use relying on conventional weapons, in
a war of nerves. In a war of nerves, nerve
is what counts. Nerve. And nerve alone.
HARKER *goes out in a state of nervous
collapse, followed by* CASK, *white-faced.*

ACT TWO

SCENE 7

*The Office. Living-room. Same.
One wall of the office, and some of the furniture, remain.*
LILIAN *enters, looks round the room with puzzled annoyance*

and misgiving, and starts rearranging the furniture. LEONARD
comes in after her, absent-mindedly helping.

LEONARD : It's in code.
  LILIAN : What's in code?
LEONARD : All of it. This. Everything. The whole
thing's in code. It's the only answer.
  LILIAN : Of course it's in code. What did you expect
it to be in?
LEONARD : What we need is a code-book.
Pause.
If we had a code-book we could get to the
bottom of all this. Tie up the loose ends.
See where it's leading to. Make sense of it
all.
Pause.
  LILIAN : If you'd left it alone in the first place.
Pause. LEONARD *wanders out to the kitchen.*
LEONARD : A meaningful overall pattern. If I could put
my finger on the code they're using.
The front doorbell rings. LILIAN *goes to
answer it.*
  LILIAN : Suddenly waking up at *this* stage and
saying it's in code.
LILIAN *comes back in, accompanied by*
HARKER.
 HARKER : Cask. Sir Francis Harker's personal
assistant. That's his card in case you
should want it. For future reference.
  LILIAN : (*reading from the card*). Timothy Cask.
 HARKER : I'm here on his behalf, actually. He's been
unavoidably detained by a 'phone call
from Scarborough—for which he asks me
to tender his apologies—and I've been
sent along from the doubles pool to

87

impersonate him. I'm not doing it very
well, I'm afraid, but you'll have to forgive
me because it's rather short notice and
I'm actually Sir Francis Harker's double.
As you can probably see.

LILIAN: Yes.

HARKER: But anyway—you must be wondering why
I'm here, Mrs. Fawcett. It really concerns
your husband. Incidentally, this wall we've
fitted you here in lieu of your own. This
is the type we're fitting now, where it's
been necessary for one reason or another
to take out an existing wall for laboratory
tests or something of that kind, because
we find it serves a useful dual purpose—in
keeping you in touch with us, and us in
touch with you. It should give you every
satisfaction, but if at any time it needs
attention, don't hesitate to give us a ring
and we'll be round as soon as ever we can
to look at it for you.

LILIAN: Yes. Thank you. We'll do that.

HARKER: Now. The thing is this, Mrs. Fawcett.
Your husband. What we've decided to do,
as he wasn't unfortunately able to find his
way to us in time for the selection board
—even though we did in fact prolong the
sitting for an extra six months to allow
him the maximum latitude for running us
to earth. . . .

LILIAN: He's never had much of a sense of
direction.

HARKER: No. Well, that isn't necessarily a
disadvantage, Mrs. Fawcett. It may even
suit our purposes, such as they are, better

that way. At any rate, what we are doing is to keep the board in being on a skeleton basis, with one member permanently on duty, on a rota system, so that should Mr. Fawcett finally make it, he can have his interview on the spot there and then to save any further delay. And in the meantime, so that should he be successful at the interview he can go into action right away, I would like, if I may, Mrs. Fawcett, to lodge a provisional briefing with you here and now for safe keeping and future reference.

LILIAN: Why yes. Of course.

HARKER: We've got a few details of the kind of equipment your husband will be needing, Mrs Fawcett, when he's finally passed by the board for the mission we've earmarked for him, (*he brings out a sheet of paper*) so perhaps we might start with that. If I could ask you to pass these on to him.

LILIAN: Yes. Of course. Just tell me what they are, and I'll see that he gets them.

HARKER: It's a great help to us when people are so co-operative, Mrs. Fawcett.

LILIAN: It's the least we can do, isn't it?

HARKER: Now. What have we got? (*He consults the paper.*) Yes. First of all, one or two small items we should like Mr. Fawcett to try and provide himself with, if I could make a note of them for you on a piece of paper. They can be got almost anywhere, but if he has any difficulty . . .

LILIAN: Will this do?

HARKER: Ah. Thank you. If he has any difficulty,

there's our own surplus stores in Armageddon Street which is bound to have them in stock. First of all, perhaps I should say that we're proposing to fly Mr. Fawcett to the other side of the Iron Curtain. What we have in mind is that once the aircraft is over enemy territory, we shall drop your husband straight through an open manhole into their sewers.

LILIAN : I see.

HARKER : That's the broad picture.

LILIAN : Does he know what to do when he gets down there?

HARKER : He'll be briefed by our man on the spot, Mrs. Fawcett, about that. The general idea is that he should systematically introduce foreign matter into the waste which is passing through the enemy's sewers, and so contaminate his effluence.

LILIAN : I'll tell him.

HARKER : Now. The things he's going to need. These are not in any special order, but (*writing them down*) he'll certainly want a cast-iron bootscraper. This is to facilitate his descent.

LILIAN : Into the . . .

HARKER : . . . manhole. Tell him to grasp it firmly with both hands on leaving the aircraft. Also an ironing board. We like our agents who go anywhere beyond the Iron Curtain to have an ironing board with them, in order if challenged to substantiate the cover story we furnish them with. Which, as you probably know, is that they are there to look into the possibility of opening up a chain of laundries in the Ukraine. What else? Bow and arrow. Standard equipment for checking wind direction and velocity on emerging from the sewers. While seemingly indulging in a perfectly innocent form of recreation. He'll also of course need to have with him a fast and up-to-date motor lawn-mower for a quick get-away. We'll just make a note of that, and . . . I really think we've got everything —except the usual billiard table. Oh—and (*writing it down*) a chandelier. To light his way through the sewers, without attracting too much unwelcome attention, while down there.

LILIAN : The billiard table. Should he go for any particular size?

HARKER : Whatever size he's used to, Mrs. Fawcett. It doesn't really matter. It's simply so that in an emergency he has something to barricade himself in his room with. And, of course, keep boredom at bay while doing so.

HARKER *goes for a small black attaché-case which he has brought with him, and which has on it an official government crest, and in gold lettering the words: "Ministry of Intelligence and Security."*

HARKER : A deciding factor, as far as size is concerned, could well be the . . . hold-all which he'll be using to carry them round in. This we provide.

LILIAN : Is there any special way of packing them in?

HARKER : Any way at all, Mrs. Fawcett, that
appears to give results. We leave that
entirely to the agent himself. In addition,
there are just two other small things. One
is this suicide capsule. If you could tell your
husband, Mrs. Fawcett, to slip it under
his dentures before he sets out. All he
needs to do then, if he feels himself giving
way under interrogation at any time, is
simply to give a slight crunch, and . . .
he's . . . (*he waves a hand*).

LILIAN : I see.

HARKER : Just common or garden cyanide, I'm
afraid—but it seems to do the trick. And
this is a detonator. The idea being to
secrete this on his person somewhere,
together with a ton and a half of nitro-
glycerine, and use it in the event of capture
to blow himself up.

LILIAN : I'll put that over here, then, with the
capsule, and we shall know where they are.

HARKER : And that, I think, Mrs. Fawcett, is about
everything.

LILIAN : Yes. Well—I'm sorry you haven't been
able to see him before you go. But I'll
certainly tell him what you've said.

HARKER : If you would, Mrs. Fawcett.
HARKER *makes his way by force of habit
towards the door leading into his office.*

LILIAN : It's half the battle, isn't it? Having the right
things.

HARKER : It is. It is indeed. Oh, yes. (*Indicating the
office wall.*) An occasional flick with the
duster, by the way. Normal care. Usual
precautions. Should last you the best part

of a lifetime.

LILIAN: Oh . . .

HARKER: Yes. Between ourselves, Mrs. Fawcett, I think we can say that the loose ends are beginning to tie up. Before very long we shall—with any luck at all—see the whole thing fall plumb into perspective.

LILIAN: Well . . . I hope it does, Mr. . . . . Cask.

HARKER: And once that happens, we can go forward in confidence at last towards ultimate victory.

LILIAN: Yes. I'm sure.

HARKER: In fact, with our backroom boys in the spearhead of our advance attack, our front men bringing up the rear, and our undercover agents standing by to go over the top, we may very well be poised, if we did but know it, for the greatest leap forward the world of counter-espionage has ever known!

LILIAN: Oh. Well—that's *very* good news, I must say.

HARKER: Yes. Well, thank you for calling, Mrs. Fawcett. Good-bye.

HARKER goes into his office and closes the door. LILIAN *stands at the other door, hovering indecisively.* HARKER'S *door opens again, and* LILIAN *bolts, closing the door behind her.* LEONARD *enters through the upstage door, carrying a pile of books.*

LEONARD: It's here, Lilian. I'm convinced of it. Somewhere in this room. If only I knew where to lay my hands on it.

He comes downstage centre and drops the books, which scatter over the floor. He

93

rummages through them in search of the missing code.

LEONARD : The one vital clue. Find that, and we can decipher the whole thing. Once and for all. Know exactly where we stand.
(*Calling.*) Eureka! (*He goes to the downstage door, opens it, and calls through.*) Lilian!
There is no reply. LEONARD *turns back into the room, closing the door again behind him, and with his eyes fixed to the piece of paper crosses slowly to the scattered books. As he does so, the door slowly vanishes behind him, leaving only blank wall where it used to be.* LEONARD *reads from the piece of paper.*
Suddenly the door was slammed, the key turned, and the light extinguished.
Blackout. LEONARD *gropes for a torch, and with it searches for another piece of paper, which he finds and reads.*
I was trapped.
He throws it down and resumes the search by the light of the torch. He finds another piece of paper, and reads it.
Before I could utter aught save a muffled curse, I was seized from behind and flung headfirst into an open grand piano, the heavy lid of which . . .
He throws it down and resumes the search as before till he finds another cutting and reads it out.
. . . was instantly closed on me. For some time I lay there stunned, not knowing what had happened.

He throws it down and repeats the business as before.

Then, like a flash, the truth dawned on me! *The lights come up. The office door has now vanished, and is replaced by blank wall.* LEONARD *stands staring for some moments at the piece of paper in his hand.* I had been poisoned.

CURTAIN